Hospitality is one of the mos
these days one of the most
from his extensive knowledge of customs in Bible times and
applies them to the present time. This book is a refreshing
reminder of how hospitality in all its forms and expressions can
be creatively restored to us. It is relevant to every Christian,
whether single or married, living alone or with others. I recom-
mend it warmly.

Lyndon Bowring

Here is a message that is especially relevant for Christians in
today's Western and individualistic culture. The book has been
carefully researched, is thoroughly biblical, offers much practical wisdom and, if acted upon, will make a significant difference
to our personal lives, as well as those of local churches and
communities.

Canon Julian Henderson, MA

To love people is to be hospitable. This book brings us back to
some really important biblical ideas. It challenges us to love
people through hospitality, and in our postmodern environment
this is a major way in which we demonstrate the truth and
wonder of Jesus. This book and its subject are vital for us at this
time.

Laurence Singlehurst, YWAM

Our house group has used this as a study book, providing a
challenging insight into Christian hospitality within a secular
community.

Mike and Jo Newton

This book has been invaluable in helping me to prepare for the strengthening of our welcome and hospitality ministry at St Michael's. The biblical background to hospitality is clearly expounded. The practical justification for investing time, energy and prayer in hospitality is convincingly made and the suggestions about how to motivate, train and organise for this ministry are extraordinarily helpful.

Christopher Talbot, St Michael's, Church of England, Paris

Angels on Your Doorstep

Hospitality in the Home, Church and Community

PADDY BERESFORD

KINGSWAY PUBLICATIONS
EASTBOURNE

First published 2004

Unless otherwise indicated, biblical quotations are
from the New International Version © 1973, 1978, 1984
by the International Bible Society.
RSV = Revised Standard Version © 1946, 1952, 1971,
1973 by the Division of Christian Education and Ministry of the
National Council of the Churches of Christ in the USA.

ISBN 1 84291 142 2

Published by
KINGSWAY COMMUNICATIONS LTD
Lottbridge Drove, Eastbourne BN23 6NT, England.
Email: books@kingsway.co.uk

Book design and production for the publishers by
Bookprint Creative Services, P.O. Box 827, BN21 3YJ, England.
Printed in Great Britain.

Contents

To Sylvia Beney

Acknowledgements

I am grateful to my wife, Ann, and our two daughters, Gabrielle and Charlotte, for being part of the shaping process in the hospitality we have sought to give over the years, and to those in three churches over 26 years (not to mention friends in other churches) who have both given hospitality and entered the discussions and ruminations that have been the foundation of this book.

I do give special thanks to all those who have run an open home that we have enjoyed from time to time and from whom we have learned much. There are too many to list, but at the risk of omissions I will make special mention of some who have continuously practised hospitality towards us, as well as those who have specifically contributed to this book (whether they realised it or not) through discussion or written submissions: Phil Arnold, Sylvia Beney, Herbert and Margaret Beresford, Mike and Pat Bigden, John and Judith Bradley, Gill and Terry Comfort, Elizabeth Corrie, Andy and Jan Harding, Andy and Pippa Harsant, Keith and Maralyn Hine, Steven and Lyn Hoyles, Graham and Irene Houston, Barry and Penny Jennings, Brian and Brenda Jones, Bill and Margaret Lubbock, Ron and Patty McCulluch, Bronek and Mandy Pomorski, Jill Rees, Herve and Jennifer Sarteau, Peter and Sheena Stredwick, Tony and Sylvia Taylor, Peter and Mac Tompsett, Jim and Helen Watkin, Ted and Barbara Watkis.

I have quoted authors of material that I have personally hunted out in the relevant areas, but I must thank all those whose names and thoughts I have been unable to recall but who have contributed to my memory and notes on these things long before I dreamed that they would materialise in book form.

Foreword

I don't like being told off. I never did. When I was a child I was very stubborn and unresponsive to anyone who tried to teach me or change my behaviour by the use of verbal or physical force. Making me feel guilty was unlikely to get anyone very far either. It is interesting to note, given this array of negative reactions, that my young soul was almost always filled to the brim with a fierce desire to be good. So what did work? The same things that work now: love, respect and cheerful willingness to take time in helping me to understand. Those were the things that did the trick. Those were the qualities that were likely to draw me from my cave and persuade me that it might be a good thing to explore wider possibilities of attitude and behaviour. Whoever offered me those wonderful things was able to hold me in the palm of their hand. I am so happy to have learned that God is like that, and it can be a real pleasure to spend time in the palm of his hand.

I have enjoyed and appreciated this book for all the same very good reasons. It is immensely refreshing to encounter a voice that speaks from the printed page with authority, compassion and more than a hint of whimsy and humour. I have only met Paddy on a couple of occasions, but I know from those encounters and from listening to those who know him well that there could not be a better person to tackle a subject that is so crucial to successful outreach by those churches and groups who genuinely want to introduce others to Jesus. And 'genuinely' is the word. As Paddy points out, we pay a great deal of lip service to the idea of evangelising through friendship, but not many of us are truly willing to let strangers and acquaintances into the centre of the real world that exists behind our castle walls. How many of us – and this is a question that Paddy's church asked themselves – know more than one or two non-Christians, often because we are so busily involved in what we have come to believe is the Lord's work? How will we respond to this challenge to open our homes and lives, and allow them to become places where friends and strangers alike will encounter the love and respect and cheerful willingness that characterise the heart of God? Is church allowed to happen in your kitchen? It can be great fun, you know!

Perhaps I shouldn't say this, but I read the last bit of the book first – the part about Abraham entertaining angels unawares. Paddy's masterful analysis of this ancient tale of the book of Genesis provides a blueprint for hospitality that entertains, inspires and challenges all at the same time. We are to welcome visitors as though we are welcoming God himself. I hurried back to the beginning of the book. So will you.

Adrian Plass

Introduction

This is a book about evangelism. 'Friendship evangelism' was a watchword of the last decade or so. Sadly, many failed to grasp the role of hospitality despite that emphasis on friendship. All sorts of activities were arranged under the banner of friendship evangelism – a round of golf, a drink at the local, a walk in the hills – but somehow, by keeping these activities outside the home, we managed to keep our homes hermetically sealed.

Yet welcoming the stranger into our home has been a biblical command from the earliest times. Perhaps part of the reason for this command was because the Jews were to be a light to the Gentiles (Old Testament description of evangelism). We will look at this in detail later.

I will also touch on the value of hospitality among fellow believers. It's theological to evangelise Christians (Romans 1:15) by sharing the good news with each other. We need companionship, and though we often find fellowship in the church building when we meet together, there remains no better substitute for deepening our relationships with one another than an invitation to meet in our homes.

These twin reasons for using our homes, evangelism and fellowship, are ancient ways laid down by God for building a neighbourhood and society that has godly roots.

I have long been exercised by the thought that our homes can be one of our most valuable tools in evangelism, and over the last few years I have been making some notes, most of which are included in this book. My wife and I have come to understand that by inviting people into our home we invite them into a place of safety and warm companionship. There's nothing more sought after in the human psyche than that basic need.

Of course, we need to go beyond the first steps of hospitality, which is probably a cup of tea and a cake, to discover that this forgotten ministry is more than a nice extra if we happen to have the time and resources for it. Hospitality is a historic, foundational response to the call to love our fellow man.

In 2 Corinthians 5:20 Paul says, 'We are therefore Christ's ambassadors, as though God were making his appeal through us . . .' He is appealing to a world that does not yet know of his love and mercy; a world where there are many who are lost, many who are searching for the meaning to life and desperate to make sense of the horrors that seem to be escalating and coming nearer and nearer to 'home'.

Paul had said earlier that Christ's love compelled him, meaning that once he realised the extent of Christ's love on the cross, that immense, unconditional love drew him, pushed him, motivated him, to live in a different way. Not for himself, not for his career or his own well-thought-out goals and ambitions, but rather to live 'for him who died . . . and was raised again'.

Living for ourselves is never a problem; living for someone else involves self-sacrifice. Of course when that person has made sacrifices for us it becomes much easier, at least for a while. But human nature ensures that we, like a magnet, soon return to a focus on ourselves. Keeping our eyes on Jesus and how he powerfully demonstrated God's love for the world is a must if we are truly going to live as those who have died to themselves.

Historically, we might make a note of the fact that those who have been unwilling to give up their lives have made no great advances for Christianity. Why are we so unwilling to give up our lives? Is it that we have never settled in our hearts that we do not live for ourselves any more?

What does it mean to live for Christ? It means that we are to be driven by a passion to find ways of telling others about Jesus. We are to be messengers of reconciliation; ambassadors for the truth. There is no British ambassador in Britain, no American ambassador in the United States. There will be no ambassadors for Jesus in heaven. We are ambassadors in a place that is 'not our home'; a place that, in the main, does not know Jesus. Moreover, there is no one else in our generation, or in our neighbourhood, other than those who follow Jesus, that is called to this work. If we fail, our neighbourhood is bereft of perhaps its only opportunity to hear about Jesus.

That realisation changed my lifestyle. For, like many other believers, I could count on one hand the unbelievers I knew well, and most didn't live within a practical distance! As a pastor my own personal evangelism was among those who came to the church because they were interested; a relatively easy step to talk to them about Jesus, and pretty safe too. I began to realise the non-Christians around me were not going to seek me out; I had to go to them. Better still, I could invite them into my home and show love and kindness towards them.

Paul said that he no longer looked at anyone from a human point of view. I had begun to learn how to do that, but predominantly within church circles. It was harmless and predictable, though some church meetings were still a challenge! If it crossed my mind that to be an ambassador was to be so *outside* the church, I saw no reasonable way of allotting time for the congregation or myself to do so. I needed people to support our busy church programme. Leaders' meetings, planning committees and prayer meetings took up all the time that we dared take from our family life.

So how could I balance it? When this lifestyle change happened, I tried but failed to reshape leaders' forums and church activities. I simply discovered what I feared; namely, how trad-itional patterns of church life have become so ingrained into our Christian culture – things like two services on a Sunday, a midweek prayer meeting, a midweek house group, a monthly church meeting, and regular leaders' meetings in order to be ready for the church meeting. If you are a leader in some churches, there's no time for evangelism, but if leaders cannot set an example in evangelism (or anything else) how can the flock follow? Our religious traditions, coupled with our British heritage of 'homes as castles', have led to a very low and some-times nil fulfilment of the command to practise hospitality. What is first needed is for the whole church to catch the vision of the call to work in the community.

The book of Acts is full of examples of the priority of those first Christians to get out into the community and evangel-ise.This action is the only real prelude to necessary meetings. Church business meetings should follow natural evangelism in the community. All too often we're bogged down with unneces-sary, habitual meetings as a prelude to the possibility of a work in the community, or finance meetings that largely consist of how we can keep the fabric going. Although we surely need to discuss and pray about such matters, *doing* the work *supported* by prayer is always going to be better than discussing the work followed by prayer.

This book is about one forgotten way of being an ambassa-dor: practising hospitality. And what better way of balancing the areas of being a family, being involved in the church and reaching unbelievers, than to see the home as part of church life and the proper fulfilment of the biblical command to reach out to the stranger, the lonely, the fatherless and the widow? Thus a family, or an individual, who practises hospitality in the com-munity experiences natural friendship evangelism.

Ambassadors look for ways of representing the people. At one of my pastorates I came to know the mayor quite well. One day he asked me whether it would be possible for him to attend our church. 'Of course. You'd always be welcome,' I said, giving him the times of the services. He replied that what he meant was to be invited to a service where he could come all dressed up, perhaps do a presentation and bring his mayoral entourage with him. He wanted to come as mayor, to be recognised (preferably by the local paper) as representing all aspects of the community. He was looking for ways to be an official ambassador. Christmas was approaching, so I encouraged him to be our guest at the candlelight service. He heard the gospel and his wife took a copy of the *Jesus* video. He'd found a way to be an ambassador to our part of the Christian community, and we'd found a way to be an ambassador of the gospel.

There is urgency contained in the commission to preach the gospel. From a broad perspective of God's message to us in the Bible we realise that we are ambassadors in a war zone. Spiritually people are dying all around us and Ezekiel 33 gives us a prod to blow the trumpet and warn the inhabitants of our nation of impending disaster. That is all true. It is a needful perspective.

On the other hand, when we consider our community, our neighbours and our work colleagues, the perspective narrows and I wonder whether we need to always be thinking, 'Blood on our heads!' For in the midst of any physical war, away from the front line, there's diplomacy, persuasion and talks going on. Who does these things? Ambassadors, envoys, government representatives.

Although the reality and the horror of war are never forgotten, a new perspective comes into play: taking time to build relationships with the enemy's envoys, earning trust, speaking plainly. All these things are important and they are done in situations that are surprisingly inconsistent with the practice of war. They are done in comfort, around tables and over meals. In fact, hospitality in some form or other is nearly always high on the agenda of diplomats.

Yes, there's urgency, but the business of friendship evangelism takes time. Yes, there is a danger in our getting too comfortable, but loving our neighbours will mean learning to be comfortable with them.

In this book I aim to explore some of the many different ways we can engage with those around us, using our home, our immediate neighbourhood, and to some extent the work place, as the platform for living out our Christian lives.

1

Ancient Customs

... for you know the heart of a stranger, for you were strangers in the land of Egypt. (Exodus 23:9 RSV)

Love of strangers

Hospitality is one of the oldest customs and duties in the Scriptures. There is no single word for it, but interestingly the New Testament word *philoxenia* means literally 'love of strangers' and this is the phrase we find in Deuteronomy 10:18 (translated as 'alien' in the NIV): 'He defends the cause of the fatherless and the widow, and loves the alien, giving him food and clothing. And you are to love those who are aliens, for you yourselves were aliens in Egypt.'

That love for strangers permeated ritual practices too: 'When you have finished setting aside a tenth of all your produce in the third year, the year of the tithe, you shall give it to the Levite, the alien, the fatherless and the widow, so that they may eat in your towns and be satisfied' (Deuteronomy 26:12).

Hospitality was specifically commanded by God (Leviticus 19:33–34). Several Old Testament personalities set a good example in the practice of hospitality. These included Abraham (Genesis 18:1–8), David (2 Samuel 6:19), the Shunammite woman (2 Kings 4:8–10), Nehemiah (Nehemiah 5:17–18), and Job (Job 31:17–20). Therefore we can say that hospitality was considered a moral pillar in many ancient civilisations; it was a

17

necessary activity to create well-being in a community and protection for strangers and travellers by providing at least food and a link into a wider circle of people.

For the early Hebrews the understanding that they were sojourners and strangers who were called upon to care for the strangers among them was part of what it meant to be a people who followed the ways of the Hebrew God. Their understanding of hospitality was not only based on God's specific command; it was also, and very significantly, endorsed by a covenantal understanding of relationship with a knowable God who promised divine blessings as a result.

The failure to offer hospitality was a breach of etiquette rarely found in the ancient East, where it was considered a sacred duty. It wasn't simply a matter of inviting the stranger in either, as it included any animals travelling with him too. This was quite an undertaking, as most travellers were not on foot and were accompanied by at least one animal. The earliest example of this is Abraham's servant on his commission to find a wife for Isaac.

> When the camels had finished drinking, the man took out a gold nose ring weighing a beka and two gold bracelets weighing ten shekels. Then he asked, 'Whose daughter are you? Please tell me, is there room in your father's house for us to spend the night?' She answered him, 'I am the daughter of Bethuel, the son that Milcah bore to Nahor.' And she added, 'We have plenty of straw and fodder, as well as room for you to spend the night.' (Genesis 24:22–25)

Such hospitality was expected. There was no awkwardness, even though sometimes it was abused (Genesis 19). It was this normal custom that Jesus expected would happen when he sent out the disciples:

> 'Take nothing for the journey except a staff – no bread, no bag, no money in your belts. Wear sandals but not an extra tunic. Whenever you enter a house, stay there until you leave that town.' (Mark 6:8)

Some feel that inviting himself for a meal at Zaccheus's house was presumptuous of Jesus, even rude, but it was culturally acceptable to do so. There are plenty of other New Testament examples showing the extent to which the practice was followed in Jesus' time: Mary (Matthew 26:6–13), Martha (Luke 10:38), the early Christians (Acts 2:45–46), Lydia (Acts 16:14–15), and Priscilla and Aquila (Acts 18:26).

Romans 12:13 reiterates the command, and the New Testament letters make a point of encouraging all believers to engage in it (1 Peter 4:9), especially church leaders (Titus 1:7–8; 1 Timothy 3:2). Jesus himself emphasised the importance of hospitality (Luke 14:13–14). He answered the question of who should inherit the kingdom of God by saying: 'I was a stranger and you invited me in' (Matthew 25:35). Even today a traditional greeting to the guests among the Bedouin people of the Middle East is 'You are among your family'.

Why was this such an important principle for God to lay down for his people? Deuteronomy 10:19 tells us, 'You are to love those who are aliens, for you yourselves were aliens in Egypt.' In other words, they had known what it was like to live in a place where they were held at arm's length, where the welcome was restrained, where they were abused, where they felt lonely and rejected. There is nothing like experience to mould lifestyle. What has become known as 'The Golden Rule' was taught by Jesus in his foundational Sermon on the Mount: 'So in everything, do to others what you would have them do to you, for this sums up the Law and the Prophets' (Matthew 7:12).

Most of us, if not all of us, will have known times when we have felt some of these emotions. Perhaps we've moved house and experienced no warmth from our new neighbours. Maybe we've asked directions while travelling to a new part of the country and been rebuffed. We may have suffered trauma or loss and not found any comfort, or worse, been held at arm's length because people have not known what to say, so they've said nothing. If you remember those feelings and have decided in your heart to learn from them and to treat others differently

when you meet them in similar situations, then you have learned
the principle that God is laying down here.

Aspects of hospitality

In Bible times, hospitality included washing the guests' feet
after they had walked a distance along hot, sandy paths and
offering refreshment by providing oil (today's deodoriser) and
a meal. The household member with the lowest rank undertook
foot-washing, or if there were household servants they would
usually do it: 'Here is your maidservant, ready to serve you and
wash the feet of my master's servants' (1 Samuel 25:41). The
account of Abraham entertaining the three angels (Genesis 18)
represents a perfect picture of the way in which a modern
Bedawee sheikh receives travellers arriving at his home.

The tension at the Passover in the upper room was caused by
the argument about which of the disciples was the greatest,
coupled with the refusal of any of them to take the lowest position and wash the feet of the others. Jesus used the occasion to
demonstrate his humility and the humility that should be dis-
played by all leaders in the kingdom of God. Indeed, Psalm 23
concludes with a picture of the Host of all hosts (God), who
prepares a table for the weary, anoints the head of the guest
with oil and shows every kindness to the extent that the guest's
cup runs over.

The parable of the Good Samaritan is probably the best-
known New Testament example of how far the provision of hospitality to a stranger can go, and it is poignantly portrayed in the
context of the 'religious' ignoring the opportunity for the same
level of ministry. It's a parable that we would do well to see as a
wake-up call for the church today in our community witness.

The salt covenant

The ancient respect for the covenant of bread and salt, or salt
alone, springs from the high regard in which hospitality was held.

As this covenant of salt plays such a central role in ancient Jewish hospitality, it would be as well to delve a little into its meaning.

God made the covenant of salt with his people as part of their worship in the temple. Salt was used with the grain offerings brought to the altar (hence the link with bread and salt): 'Season all your grain offerings with salt. Do not leave the salt of the covenant of your God out of your grain offerings' (Leviticus 2:13). In Numbers 18:19 God allows the priests to eat a share of these holy offerings. It was symbolic of God's commitment to his priests, for it was to be 'an everlasting covenant of salt before the Lord for both you and your offspring'.

Salt is a symbol of holiness, purity, cleanliness and longevity. A covenant of salt between God and his people, through the priesthood, was to be a seal of a good, healthy, long-lasting relationship. The fact that such offerings were presented in the temple (where the sacrifice for sin was made) before Almighty God was to be a sign that the people were willing to put right anything that was wrong in their relationship with the Lord. This picture was acted out in the homes of the Israelites, not only as a symbol of their right relationship with God, but as a sign of good relationships within the family and with others outside. So 'eating salt together' was a part of many meals.

At a Jewish meal, salt was always present. Just as a bowl of water was positioned on every table for hand-washing, so salt was there for a number of reasons. First and foremost, particularly since the destruction of the temple, the table was seen as an altar. So as Harvey Lutske notes, 'When we make the benediction over bread, we add salt as a symbolic sacrifice.'[1]

In fact the Hebrew word for bread (*lechem*) has the same Hebrew letters as the Hebrew word for salt (*melech*), underlining this link. Salt was harvested from the Dead Sea, but it was also produced in the process of kosher cooking through extracting blood from meat. This process naturally created salt for the sacrifice and the meal, so that when there was food enough to eat, the salt was a reminder that their history included times of austerity and that food was a divine provision.

In New Testament terms, the matter of God allowing the priests to partake of this grain and salt offering is now transferred to us (1 Peter 2:5, 9), although it was God's intention that all Israel would be priests right from the start (Exodus 19:6). Priestly duties include forgiveness towards one another and, interestingly, evangelism: 'the priestly duty of proclaiming the gospel of God' (Romans 15:16).

Jesus used salt as a picture of what Christians are to be to the world: rubbed in (not distant), preserving (not ignoring), healing and soothing (salt, not pepper!). If we are to be salt to our non-Christian communities then there will be the absolute necessity to be right with one another. And there's nothing like hospitality in sharing a meal together with our fellow believers to safeguard and perpetuate that good fellowship.

The meal in ancient Israel was an opportunity to express forgiveness to one another

So, Hebrew history informs us that hospitality has a wealth of meaning for our Christian lives today. The meal in ancient Israel was an opportunity to express forgiveness to one another by 'eating salt together' and it fulfilled the command to practise hospitality to the stranger, which was a means of being a 'light to the Gentiles'. Today we take up that baton, and the practice of hospitality becomes an opportunity to proclaim all the truths and facets of the kingdom of God.

The Greek background

The Greek background is slightly different. There is no personal, illustrative appeal to hospitality as in Hebrew history: 'as you were once strangers, so welcome the stranger'. Rather it is more calculated and seen as a 'proper' thing to do: 'Rudeness to a stranger is not decency, poor though he may be . . . all wanderers and beggars come from Zeus. What we can give is slight but the recompense great.'[2] What we observe here is the dubious basis of benefit and reciprocity in relationship-forming which has stepped up a gear with the twenty-first-century practice of networking in the Western world. The deduction is that only if a relationship can better your standing in the community, business or even the church, is it worth the effort of offering hospitality. This is far removed from the teaching of the Scriptures, and particularly the teaching of Jesus, that hospitality stretches first and foremost to the weak and needy and those least able to reciprocate.

Because the West builds its philosophy of life on Greek ways rather than Hebrew ones, it is important to recognise these differences. Looking at ancient Greek society and Homer in particular, we find that Homer divided society into two types: the savage and the hospitable. Greece was very proud of its hospitality to strangers, although at first it treated them with reserve and there were specific boundaries. For instance, they were granted no rights, at least initially. It was, however, a religious perspective: strangers were placed under the protection of Zeus, and their rights were gradually defined as they settled into the new world.

Zeus was the chief god of the ancient Greeks and ruler of the heavens. Through this relationship, strangers, foreigners or travellers were regarded as guests of the deity and therefore their sanctuaries were the primary places of hospitality. Out of this emerged the need for hospices and inns, which were often linked with temples, synagogues or places of pilgrimage.

Mistreatment of strangers was a serious offence. Greek society was encouraged to cultivate an ethic that reflected an attitude of welcome. There may have been no rights to begin with, but this was balanced by hospitality, which was viewed as a distinctive of civilised society. Interestingly, Stoicism taught that there was a relationship between the divine and the human because we are all world citizens and therefore there can be no strangers.

Despite the Hebrew and Greek traditions it has to be said that Christians have often been slow to embrace these ideals. From the Greeks have come two words that illustrate Homer's two aspects of society: *xenophilia* (loving the stranger) and *xenophobia* (fearing the stranger, which led to the more savage treatment of them). These two worldviews emerge through history as strands with huge swings in thought and practice. In the West it has emerged largely as an anxiety to protect ourselves from the influences of other religions and cultures. In the East there has been a greater acknowledgement of hospitality as an important cultural feature of society, but as stronger divisions occur between East and West that threaten war and have political and economic agendas, there's a growing suspicion of strangers.

Jesus shocked his observers through continuous expressions of hospitality.

This is not an entirely new phenomenon: Josephus and Philo encouraged notions of inclusion and acceptance, yet resisted them in practice, I suspect due to more primitive fears. For all sorts of reasons, fear of neighbours who are different comes much more naturally to people than loving them.

The Christian community has also tended to reveal a dislike for things foreign. Yet the gospel is based on the life of one who taught that the heart of God contained a huge capacity for *xenophilia* and not *xenophobia*: to show love towards the stranger rather than fear of the stranger.

Jesus shocked his observers through continuous expressions of hospitality and by showing the kind of love that is capable of casting out all fear. He also established new and revolutionary benchmarks for loving our neighbours, the unlovable, the unacceptable and even our enemies.

Lactantius, the emperor Constantine's family tutor, contrasted the Christian approach to hospitality, as he had learned it, with a non-Christian approach. His belief was that hospitality was a 'principle virtue' and he strongly criticised those who would practise hospitality for advantage, drawing attention to the ideas of Marcus Cicero, a well-known Roman orator (106–43 BC), who thought that the houses of distinguished men should be open to distinguished guests. Lactantius argued that the house of a 'just' man ought not to be open to the illustrious, but to the lonely and abject, 'for those illustrious and powerful men cannot be in want of anything'.[3] Lactantius went on to explain that this didn't mean that entertaining friends and neighbours was out of the question, but the former was the 'true and just work'.

The early Christian writers claimed that they bridged social differences, and sometimes ethnic differences, by sharing their homes and eating meals with people from backgrounds different from their own. John Chrysostom in the fourth century apparently insisted that hospitality should be face to face, gracious, unassuming, indiscriminate and always enthusiastic.

PUTTING PRINCIPLES INTO PRACTICE

1. 'You are to love those who are aliens, for you yourselves were aliens in Egypt' (Deuteronomy 10:18). Have you ever lived or worked in a place where you have been held at arm's length and, as a result, felt lonely and rejected? Discuss what emotions were present.

2. 'The Golden Rule' (Matthew 7:12) is a foundational teaching of the Sermon on the Mount. How much does this teaching form the backbone of your lifestyle? What factors might cause you to shy away from practising it?

3. What part does reciprocation play in any hosting that you may do?

4. The twenty-first-century practice of networking, to better opportunities or status, has become widespread. How do you feel when relationships are sought on this basis at a party or a church function? How might you go out of your way to engage with someone who is not 'fitting in' at such a function?

5. What, if any, aspects of 'eating salt together' have a place at our tables today?

6. Begin making a list of people you know are lonely or alone and pray for them, asking God what you might do to help.

2
Starting Relationships

From quiet homes and first beginning,
Out of the undiscovered ends,
There's nothing worth the wear of winning,
But laughter and the love of friends.

(Hilaire Belloc, 'Dedicatory Ode')

A welcoming community

Let's face it, most British communities are not the best example of welcome that this world offers. It is embarrassing to compare the welcome of even our smallest communities with the welcome one would experience in other parts of the world, especially the developing world. I have had the privilege of trav-elling in Africa, eastern Europe and Asia, and would conclude that there seems to be a 'contrary scale' evidenced by the fact that the poorer the household the more gener-ous the welcome.

Sadly, much of our so-called hospitality is an excuse to show off what we have or what we do.

In Britain we like the security of our fences and of shut doors much more than open doors and neighbourliness. I suspect the history is rooted in imperialism, one-upmanship and misplaced pride. Catchphrases like 'keeping up with the Joneses' and 'keeping up appearances' have become part of our culture. If this is the motivation of our lives there is little hope for welcoming the stranger, the needy and the lonely – at least, not on the basis of empathy. Sadly, much of our so-called hospitality is an excuse to show off what we have or what we do.

26

Moving on

From the moment someone moves into a new community there is a need for them to experience a welcome. Therefore, in order to consider how good relationships start, I shall begin with the arrival of the newcomer.

Sale boards

Sale boards around the community are often the first sign that people are moving on. Sadly, it's often the signal to bemoan the fact that 'we didn't really know them' or 'we often spoke of having them round'. If that is the case, why not make a real effort for the new people? Make a mental note to get a welcome card. We've just undertaken our seventh move and were particularly touched by one local family who took the trouble to make their own welcome card, with each of the three children adding their own designs or ideas. If there's a gap between the previous owners leaving and the new arriving, it might be possible to keep the lawn mowed and the garden tidy. Be imaginative: no one has to be super-creative or have oodles of time to spare; just thinking of a few simple things to make the new people welcome will be better than no thought at all.

The vendor's farewell

If you are the one who is moving, there's something you can do to make the people who are moving in feel welcome. Apart from cleaning the house properly, you too can leave a welcome card. In fact, when we have moved, we have always left a bottle of wine or vase of flowers with a card, and we know this has been appreciated. Before our last move, the vendors sent us a video of the interior of every room, showing the position of the plugs, telephone points, windows, doors, radiators and thermostats. We were a three-hour drive away so, as you can imagine, this was immensely helpful and ensured that planning what we could fit in was made many times easier. Their thoughtful help meant that much of the practical side of the move went well.

Church information

Sale boards should also be a signal to the local churches to arrange to have a visitor call with a ready-prepared brochure outlining the activities of all the local churches. Such a brochure demonstrates a unity among the churches, which in itself is a sign of welcome. This, I believe, is preferable to a single church 'going it alone' with their own brochure, which might appear pushy, though obviously it is better than nothing if other churches don't want to participate. I was involved in such a joint scheme in Sussex, and the intake among the churches from people who had just moved into the area was very high, particularly among young families and singles.

The move itself

We all know that moving house is one of the most stressful activities of our modern world. Yet it is one of life's great opportunities to practise hospitality and to be a blessing to the stranger. During our seven moves we have experienced both the 'lows' of unfriendliness and suspicion and the 'highs' of tea and cake at suitable intervals. It's such an easy thing to do but it will speak louder than any verbal welcome.

Some people hire a van and move themselves, so there's an added opportunity if you are fit and free on the day of the move to roll up your sleeves and help. If you are handy at DIY, perhaps you can offer your services. Most people have a need to fix something up quickly, but it can be stressful when the tools for the job are in some packing box in an unknown place.

If the previous owner left a bottle of wine but the corkscrew is nowhere to hand it can be an anticlimax. Most of us will have experienced such frustrating scenarios. Again the offer to provide whatever might be needed until items are found is a great way of making people feel at home immediately.

Welcoming people from different ethnic backgrounds

Sadly, even those who claim not to be racist can demonstrate suspicion towards new neighbours for no other reason than the colour of their skin. Some years ago when we put our house on the market there was a definite lobby for us not to sell to an Asian family. It's not a lobbying we gave in to, but it raised for us the whole question of the kind of welcome some people receive when they move.

Those from different ethnic backgrounds will therefore often start with an added stress factor when they move and should consequently be the subject of a more concerted effort by those in their neighbourhood to welcome them. It is time to learn to celebrate the differences in culture rather than to choose to be distant and complain that their presence somehow weakens the status of the community. If a white person were moving into their country, the welcome they would receive would quite probably be of a high standard and no coldness would be perceived at all.

Hospitality: an ice-breaker

Any form of welcome is going to be an effective ice-breaker for the newcomer in a community, and hospitality in the conventional sense (i.e. a meal in the home) is a valuable way of starting relationships with others whether or not they are new to the area. I remember one of my assistants starting work at the church where I was a pastor for some years in Surrey. He had moved from Suffolk, coming from a smaller, close-knit community, and now he and his wife found themselves in a suburban road near the town centre. Even though he was the newcomer, he wanted to initiate the building of new relationships and started with his immediate neighbours in the road. When he knocked on his nearest neighbour's door to invite her in for coffee sometime over the next few days, she went to fetch her diary and stated that the next free slot would not be for at least three months! Whether it was a delaying tactic to see what sort of neighbours they would be, or whether she and her husband were genuinely busy was actually never established, as the get-together never took place. That example is not too unusual in the south east and sadly confirmed to my young associate that the area was lacking in hospitality.

One of the key words linked to hospitality is 'availability'. Hospitality just doesn't compute if time is not sacrificed for it. A slot in our diary that is several weeks or months away might be appropriate for a business meeting or a meeting with distant friends, but it is not altogether appropriate for neighbours. If we're serious about building relationships with our neighbours, then we need to be available for them. For them to pop in for a cup of tea does not take that long, and that first half an hour may be the beginning of something extremely precious.

The reason why some people are put off giving hospitality is because they feel they haven't much to offer: their home is untidy and they don't have the time to spruce it up for the 'visit'; they don't possess 'best china' or 'best cutlery'; they can't afford to cook a good meal. None of these reasons is really valid with respect to Christian hospitality. In the first place every Christian has something to offer – a welcoming smile, a care for and an interest in others – and this is a huge 'something' to people who either expect nothing or expect to be paraded around the neighbour's possessions. It's called 'being real', and it's a rare but much sought-after quality. If you are happy to be real, then there's no need to present the house in any condition other than that which you are comfortable to live in yourself. For the same reason, what you serve your food on and what you eat with is of little consequence: hospitality is centred on warm-heartedness and a demonstration that you care. To understand that makes it within reach of everyone.

> *Hospitality just doesn't compute if time is not sacrificed for it.*

Hospitality in the local church

The fellowship of the church, in the worldwide sense, is about God's people giving and receiving each other warmly and openly. It's where we take each other's hand and share the peace and strength of Christ with each other in good times and bad.

The church, Paul tells us, is the body of Christ, and the local church is the local expression of this. It is a group of believers learning to become disciples of Jesus and the company of people where we are accepted when we get it right and when we get it wrong. It is these people who should be able to challenge us yet stand by us, pick us up when we fall, bandage our sore wounds and carry us until we can walk again. It's where we feel at home and therefore where all the ingredients of good hospitality are present.

When I say that church is where we learn to be disciples of Jesus, I mean it's where we can express to each other and to the unbelieving how a gathering of ordinary people differing from each other in every way can be brothers and sisters in Christ because Christian family ties transcend all boundaries.

People have often said to me that you don't have to go to church to be a Christian, but just as a burning coal returns to coldness when removed from other burning coals, so we lose something of the fire within us when we remove ourselves from the presence of other believers. But more than this, to be the church that is described somewhat sketchily above, it is necessary for it to be done in person.

From time to time I enjoy watching the BBC's *Songs of Praise* at home, but it is not the same as being at church. Being there in person, we come face to face with other believers and become a part of God's intention of hospitality. When we are in the church building, we hear the worship of God's people raised in song all around us to lift our spirits for the week ahead, as surely as if someone had grabbed our hand and transported us to a place of beauty and a source of renewed energy (whatever the quality of the music!). We're not joining with a group of perfect people, but a selection of the world's imperfect people who need God's love and have dared to admit it.

We meet together not just for ourselves, but because together we are the body of Christ, and the roles each member of the body plays enable us to find fulfilment, as each gift not only complements the others but completes the channel of blessing that God has designed for us. So we meet together because God needs us to be there for one another, and that includes the stranger who walks through the doors for the first time. That person may be seeking God, perhaps hoping to find a different spirit from the world, and probably wanting friendship and understanding so that they are no longer alone on life's journey. If what they are looking for is not provided because you decided not to be there with the role God has given you, then the body is lame and will not be able to fulfil its task adequately. Hospitality is one of the gifts given to this body of people, though the principle applies to many other aspects of meeting together.

In this environment, God can reach out through our words and our company just as the host can reach out to visitors and strangers by welcoming them to his house. We are the ones who prepare the feast on God's behalf, who refresh thirsty travellers on God's behalf, who open our imperfect homes and imperfect hearts to other imperfect souls who would find shelter and guidance for the journey. Each of us is such a traveller and in various ways a stranger, and to others a potential angel.

If church becomes the meeting of believers alone, then we've missed a major part of God's heart for the church.

We know that love for other believers should be one of the first signs of the new life in Christ (1 John 5:1). But if church becomes the meeting of believers alone, then we've missed a major part of God's heart for the church. I have been a visitor in some churches and felt more uncomfortable than when starting a new job. The worst expression of church must be an inhospitable body of believers evidenced by a series of closely gathered groups of friends around the church who ignore new people. This might be compounded by a leadership who, when they stand up to address the congregation, assume that everyone present knows who they are and what they're talking about.

If the local church, in its various gatherings, is to be hospitable, certain foundational practices need to be addressed.

The welcome team

In my experience as a pastor, the welcome that newcomers receive is of paramount importance. A team of dedicated welcomers who are trained to notice visitors and make them feel at home should be part of every church's policy. Who needs training to smile and shake hands with people, you may ask? In the first place, it's amazing how many church welcomers don't know how to smile. OK, they may have just had an argument with someone, or feel worried about work the following day, but this is precisely why training needs to be given about being there on time, putting aside every feeling and emotion that may jeopardise good welcoming and seeing the task of welcoming as a divinely inspired way of 'being Jesus' to the newcomer. There are a few other matters to be taken into consideration too.

Appearance

Appearance does need to be addressed. I'm not talking so much about how smart the clothes are, but how they're worn. I have witnessed welcomers who look as if they rolled out of bed a quarter of an hour earlier. It doesn't concern me whether the smile I receive is broad or minimalist, but it does bother me whether or not breakfast can still be seen when the smile breaks!

Badges

A badge indicating that you are a welcomer is most helpful. Some say it's too American for the British church, but people are used to it these days, whether at business conferences or McDonald's. Badges are useful: they remind your friends that you have a job to do and mustn't be distracted, and they inform the visitor that you are the fount of at least some knowledge as to what might transpire during the service.

Welcomers are not the only ones who might benefit from wearing badges; other duty stewards and duty counsellors who are available after the service would do well to wear them.

Identifying visitors

Those in the welcome team need to be able to identify newcomers and spend time ensuring they know what to expect during the service. This means that meeting your friends and telling them the latest gossip needs to be postponed to another time, because 'on duty' welcomers have things to address for the duration of the service. People who cannot attend regularly should not be on the welcome team because a prerequisite is that the team is able to recognise who's been before (there will be plenty of other opportunities to serve for irregular attendees). Again, because of this fundamental requirement, the team members should do a month at a time rather than having different people on the door each week. A church that operates the latter scheme will find any visitors are assumed to be first-time visitors until the people who saw them the first week are on duty again! Although this may be more convenient for the welcome team, we should consider what is best for the visitor. A team that is on duty a month at a time can follow through the first welcome very well, and for the visitor it's an immediate familiar face.

Sensitivity

A warm welcome and not a smothering one is a delicate balance that needs to be learned. The body language and verbal response to a welcome is usually the best indicator as to whether a visitor is happiest creeping in the back because they're quietly 'sussing you out' or whether they need more information to help them settle.

The vast majority of visitors expect more than the basics. However, at some places I've visited, I have been met by a barrage of questions: Is this your first time? Where do you live?

What do you do? One question, well chosen and not too personal, is enough. It is also unhelpful to launch into a personal history, however 'potted' it may be.

Children

Visitors with children like to know what arrangements there are for them. They will want to know at what point in the service the children go to a class, where the class is and whether it's possible for them to stay with babies. It's a good idea to ask someone (not a welcomer) to introduce them to a family with children of a similar age.

Orientation

If badges are worn, it is easier for a visitor to be orientated. There's nothing more frustrating for a visitor than having to search for someone who might give information on things like the location of the toilets. I remember visiting one church and asking someone who was not engaged in conversation where the toilets were. But it produced the embarrassing discovery that he too was a visitor and had no idea. So he too was on his own because welcoming was not a priority. I found the toilets at the third attempt.

It's not just the average visitor who needs to know these things: young families with babies may need to change a nappy at short notice; the elderly or disabled may be reluctant to visit a new church for fear of not being able to find the toilet quickly. So welcomers need to be alert to these needs.

Most churches have a weekly bulletin or newsletter. This can be used to highlight salient points like any special events during the service. Is it communion? Explain what usually happens so that they are prepared. Is a visitor required to put their hand up because they're new? Are there other things they need to be prepared for? Are refreshments served halfway through the service, at the beginning or at the end? Might they be expected to break into discussion groups during the service? Are visitors usually given the opportunity to have lunch with someone afterwards?

Introductions

I have discovered that most newcomers are pleased to be introduced to others who live near them; it's an obvious link for building neighbourhood relationships. Again, be sensitive to whether or not you do this on the first visit. If your conversation thus far has produced a visible 'backing off', it is best to leave other introductions to another time. Certainly on a second visit introductions are a crucial aspect to the hospitality process. Introductions to an area small group leader or area pastor may also be appropriate.

A welcoming church leadership

I believe church leaders play an important role in welcoming new people. Without wanting to make too big an issue of it, I personally favour the pastor doing the welcome from the front of the church, or reiterating the welcome in some way, for a number of reasons:

- It enables newcomers to identify the pastor should they want to speak to him or her afterwards.
- The pastor is like the parent in the home. When my children bring their friends home, the welcome for that friend is always stronger when the parent does the welcoming.
- The pastor's example in all matters sets the tone for the whole church. If the pastor can welcome well and sensitively, others will do so.

The hospitality team

This is made up of people who offer hospitality in the home, usually lunch after the service. There is something very special about this. Most newcomers, unless they are brought by someone else, are either believers who are new to the area, or people who have come because they believe their sense of loneliness or lostness might be resolved by going to church. In both cases the offer of such hospitality is an enormous and valuable demonstration of love for the stranger. Pohl notes that for the early Christian community 'the church as the household of God was a powerful theological and social reality . . . Early Christian hospitality was offered from within this overlap of household and church.'[1] I found from looking at religious websites that most Jewish synagogues run hospitality teams, but I found few Christian churches advertising this service. Here is one such notice on a website for a synagogue in the States:

> Congregation Ezra Bessaroth was formed to offer aid and assistance to the needy from our community. The hospitality committee arranges for meals to be provided to Ezra Bessaroth families during serious illness. The committee provides meals to families after a birth. The committee also arranges for meals during times of illness or (G-d forbid) death. The hospitality committee visits the ill of our community when able and sends flowers and kind wishes to our members in the hospital. The hospitality committee encourages an ever growing sense of family and community. As a means towards this end the committee plans regular Family Style Shabbat Dinners. These warm, relaxed Shabbat meals have become a popular activity for the entire congregation. Should you know of anyone in the Ezra Bessaroth Community who is ill or in the hospital, please contact the Synagogue office.[2]

There is a French Yiddish proverb which says, '*L'amour est bien, mais l'amour avec des nouilles est beaucoup mieux.*' ('Love is good, but love with noodles is much better.')

Follow up

I had a policy that every newcomer should receive a written letter that expressed how good it was to welcome them to our church. This was sent the week after their visit with a personal call by someone after the second visit. I never discovered anyone complaining that we were too pushy. If the newcomer had just moved into the area, a leader, usually me, would make a house call after the first visit, because any contact with people in the locality is usually well received after moving house. That pastoral visit would include a prayer for the family as they settle – that the new house would be home and that the peace of Jesus would rest there.

Obviously such follow up has to be undertaken sensitively. It should be non-threatening and non-invasive, and it should be short unless you are encouraged to stay longer. The purpose is to welcome, give some basic information of the church (it's helpful to leave literature about services, youth work, children's work and a résumé of the church's vision and *raison d'être*) and to pray with them, unless you sense that that would not be welcome.

PUTTING PRINCIPLES INTO PRACTICE

1. Think of experiences that you may have had in feeling welcome when you moved into the area. Has that made you make others feel welcome?
2. Does your church or local Churches Together have a brochure to welcome newcomers? If not, why not design one together and ask your church leader to adopt it in the church or seek its adoption in the local group of churches?
3. How do you react when a new neighbour is from an ethnic minority group? What other attitudes are you likely to find among your neighbours? In what ways could you make a biblical attitude towards the stranger have influence in the neighbourhood?
4. Describe how you have felt when visiting another church, perhaps when on holiday. What made you feel welcome? What made you feel like an outsider. What do *you* do to make newcomers at church feel at home?
5. Have you ever invited a church visitor home for a meal afterwards? If not, do you think you might start doing so? Give your reasons.

3

Building Relationships

If a man does not make new aquaintance as he advances through life, he will soon find himself alone. A man, Sir, should keep his friendship in constant repair.

(Samuel Johnson, *Boswell's Life of Johnson*, April 1755)

The intrinsic value of our home

Trying to grasp the importance of hospitality without understanding the true value of 'home', indeed the problem of homelessness, is almost impossible. For it is out of an understanding of what the home means to us that we can estimate the value of hospitality for those who, for one reason or another, do not have a home. That is not to say that they don't have a place to live; it is to say that where they live is not home.

The place we call home is normally understood to be a place of safety. Emotions are attached to this place; we might even call it a sentimental place in the sense that it contains many of the sentiments that we have concerning our life and the living of it. Home is where we are settled, and because we are settled we feel at liberty to be ourselves. That thought has both positive and negative truths attached to it. The negative associations are voiced when we say things like, 'Who can tell what goes on behind closed doors?' But let us consider the positive facets of this place that is our settled existence. Home is where, after a long, stressful day, we can find solace in close relationships; we can 'chill out' in front of the TV, wear what is comfortable, say what we really think and do what we really like doing.

39

The Greek word for home is *oikos* and, says Lucien Richard, it 'expresses one of the most fundamental social, economic, political and personal realities of the ancient world. It describes house as home, the place where I belong. Where I have rights and obligations.'[1] The Greek verb from this noun means 'to inhabit' or 'permanently reside'. We use all kinds of different phrases that sum up home for us: 'Home is where the heart is'; 'There's no place like home'. When someone is away from home and feeling 'homesick' we can identify with those feelings. When 'ET' in the film of that name points a finger into outer space and says pathetically 'home', we are drawn to this little figure and give it personality because we understand the sentiment.

If, as Lucien Richard says, home has a social, economic, political and personal reality, then homelessness is socially, economically, politically and personally disastrous. Moreover, because the homeless person can no longer identify with the normal aspects of home, they are often made to feel outcasts who are held in suspicion because all forms of instability are perceived as a threat to society. Rosemary Haughton comments: 'Homeless people . . . don't fit in and their "not belonging" is a threat to the sense of stability everyone wants.'[2]

Understanding the dynamics of homelessness draws us to our Christian responsibility to work towards resolving the social issues that surround it. But homelessness also focuses our attention on the call that John the Baptist identified as a founding principle of the kingdom of God: to share what we have with those who lack (Luke 3:11). If our home is valued in the way that has been outlined above, then those things are to be shared. John the Baptist specifically mentions sharing food in this passage.

The value of eating together

For Christians, sharing a meal together has a special significance, because one of the pertinent issues that Jesus faced with his opponents was who you could eat with. Jesus broke with the Jewish tradition of table fellowship and ate with people who were 'unclean', demonstrating that there really is something intimate and theological about eating together.

Jesus also compared the kingdom of God to a 'messianic banquet', a veritable feast where those invited would come from every tongue, tribe and nation. It was something he looked forward to and he encouraged his disciples to live in the light of that day. Jesus even promised at the Passover meal prior to his crucifixion – the meal we now call the Last Supper – that he wouldn't drink wine again until that banquet when he would drink it with all Christians at the end of the age.

> *'God Himself is in our home, is being fed at our house, is lying down and resting.'*

In the Reformation period, Martin Luther wrote about persecuted believers receiving hospitality. At these times, he wrote, 'God Himself is in our home, is being fed at our house, is lying down and resting.'[3] The first leaders of Israel happily ate and drank in the presence of God: 'they saw God, and they ate and drank' (Exodus 24:11).

In addition to the fellowship aspects of food and religion, many faiths have specific and symbolic traditions about food associated with various celebrations and observances. For example, devout Roman Catholics usually abstain from eating meat on Fridays and instead have fish. Lent, the 40-day period between Ash Wednesday and Easter, is observed by many Christians as a period of penitence and fasting, even if it hasn't been practised for the rest of the year. Jews include the traditional sweet cakes made with honey in their Rosh Hashanah menus to symbolise sweetness and happiness for the New Year. Or they might have apples dipped in honey, symbolic of a well-rounded year ahead. And the food at Passover, placed around the Seder dish, is symbolic of different aspects of the Exodus story. Indeed all the Jewish feasts are steeped in symbolism, reminding them of their heritage.

The Christian community has systematically weakened the rich heritage of these feasts, with the result that we are deprived of the major reasons for celebration in our Christian lives. For instance, the Passover meal becomes a little piece of bread and a sip of wine that may last as long as ten minutes, often tagged on to the end of a service, and rarely gives an opportunity for any relationship-building. The 'Lord's Supper', the 'Lord's Table', 'communion' or 'Eucharist' are all terms used in the Christian faith to describe this Christianised version of the Passover meal. The little piece of bread or wafer is called 'the host' in the Anglican and Roman Catholic traditions, as it is, or symbolises, the body of Jesus, who was the host at the Last Supper. It is so symbolic that we often forget that it once involved basic foods. In fact, because the majority of the early church were Jews, the beginnings of this Christian celebration was really a meal, like a Passover, where in their homes they broke bread together as part of the meal. It also included a game for children, hunting for any leaven in the house. But our 'communion' is most solemn, and all thoughts of feasting and an opportunity for social interaction have sadly been removed.

Likewise Sukkot has become a token activity of drawing attention to some fruit, or worse still some tinned 'veg', at a harvest service. There may be some extra flowers and a weaved bunch of corn made in baker's dough, but it's hardly the celebration that is encouraged in the Scriptures.

For this reason, at one of my pastorates we often broke into small groups of six to ten during a communion service. This gave an opportunity to share and pray together and take more time over the partaking of the bread and wine. The fact that we met in a school made this easier, as the chairs were easily moved. We also encouraged house groups to celebrate communion together in their homes as the Scriptures encourage us to do (Acts 2:46). I realise that this is difficult in some Christian traditions, but it is worth approaching your vicar or priest to see what possibilities there may be of fulfilling this scriptural practice.

Christians have added other symbols to remind them of certain events, for instance Shrove Tuesday is similar to Mardi Gras (Fat Tuesday). Originally the church would gather to eat pancakes, fellowship together and celebrate before Lent. The ceremony traces its roots to pre-Reformation days, when Christians were expected to prepare for Lent by confessing their sins (the old English word is 'shriven', where the name 'shrove' comes from). Later, the bell that once called the faithful to be 'shriven' or 'penitent' became the Pancake Bell, the signal for pancakes to be made. Centuries ago, women ran through the streets tossing pancakes in a frying pan, racing to the church, the winner being the first with an intact pancake.

In numerous instances in biblical history, when two parties entered into an agreement they shared a meal together. One of the most well-known is when the herdsmen of Gerar quarrelled with Isaac's herdsmen:

> 'Let us make a treaty with you that you will do us no harm, just as we did not molest you but always treated you well and sent you away in peace. And now you are blessed by the LORD.' Isaac then made a feast for them, and they ate and drank. Early the next morning the men swore an oath to each other. (Genesis 26:28–31)

The covenant meal sealed their peaceful relationship. Another example, not so much a covenant but to seal an act of kindness, appears in 2 Samuel 9:7 where King David shows Mephibosheth, Saul's grandson, kindness:

> 'I will surely show you kindness for the sake of your father Jonathan. I will restore to you all the land that belonged to your grandfather Saul, and you will always eat at my table.'

The covenant of all covenants is the one Jesus makes with those who believe in him; a covenant that is sealed in his blood: 'This cup is the new covenant in my blood' (Luke 22:20). This is accompanied by an invitation to join in a covenant meal with him: 'Here I am! I stand at the door and knock. If anyone hears my voice and opens the door, I will come in and eat with him, and he with me' (Revelation 3:20).

In numerous instances in biblical history, when two parties entered into an agreement they shared a meal together.

Eating food is more than just a physical activity. It has an important social aspect. Eating with family and friends binds us together; it strengthens trust and acceptance of each other; it develops good conversation skills and provides an opportunity to build a sense of belonging and peace with each other. The opposite is also true, for if we are not at peace with those at the table, the pleasure is diminished. The great success of the Alpha course is largely to do with the provision of a meal before any teaching and discussion takes place. It underlines the felt needs of many people. Eating together is a valuable tool for building relationships.

Mealtimes are at risk in our modern society. The very act of sitting round a table together as a family, sharing relaxed conversation, is a special thing, but eating in silence in front of the TV is often the norm. Perhaps we are returning to our hunter-gatherer instincts! Peter Farb has said:

> Because food is essential for all human beings, offering it to someone is usually considered to be a 'pure gift' . . . When the Arctic explorer, Peter Freuchen, was given meat by Eskimos with whom he had been living, he thanked them, as he had been trained to do at home. An old man promptly corrected him: 'You must not thank for your meat; in this country, nobody wishes to be dependent on others. Therefore, there is nobody who gives or gets gifts, for thereby you become dependent. With gifts you make slaves just as with whips you make dogs.' Thanking anyone for food is a serious breach of etiquette among hunter-gatherers because it implies both that the giver is not generous as a matter of course and that he is not a good enough hunter to afford to give away meat. More important, by his thanks the recipient seems to deny the obligation to repay at some future date. A hunter shares because it is the appropriate thing to do in his society; he later expects to receive, and this

is his right. The well-brought-up recipient in a hunting-gathering society praises the giver for his hunting prowess but never for his generosity. [4]

Thankfulness, in Christian homes, should be part of a shared meal: we give thanks before eating with a 'grace', and then during the meal we often thank each other in various ways for preparing, cooking or coming. It's the basic etiquette of sharing food together around the table. Donald Altman, a former Buddhist monk, reminds us that most actions can be undertaken at either a surface level or in a deeper, more thoughtful and meaningful way. He says, 'Eating with awareness brings us into the moment, helps us understand what it means to be alive, and connects us to the mystery and source of all living things. Food can even unlock the door to our most personal, treasured memories.'[5] Most of us can think back to some special meals (Christmas, birthdays or picnics), and in recalling these moments relive the emotions we experienced.

> *'Eating with awareness . . . helps us understand what it means to be alive, and connects us to the mystery and source of all living things.'*

Most religions have times for community feasting. Hinduism uses a creative artform called 'Rangoli', which is mainly painted on the ground in front of people's houses using different coloured powders to welcome guests during Diwali. Muslims celebrate Eid to mark the end of a month-long fast during the month of Ramadan. 'Eid' means 'recurring happiness' or 'festivity'. Muslims from all strata of life can be seen adorned in beautiful new clothes. It is a time of celebration and hospitality; a time to forget old grudges and ill feelings towards others and an opportunity to give to the needy.

Judaism, as we have seen, has many opportunities for communal eating. There is the weekly Sabbath meal, and an annual meal, the Passover, that celebrates how the Jewish people came

to be. The form of the Passover meal involves the telling of the
story of the Jews – of how Moses led them out of bondage
in Egypt. Specific foods come to symbolise Jewish life, and the
storytelling of the Passover creates a communal identity.

The church today is often heard to be searching for models
of a more authentic Christian life, where the true core of
kingdom living can be seen. Generally the non-Christian community around us is tired of words; they want to see Christian
truth practised in such a way that the choice between the
kingdom of God and the kingdom of darkness is clearly presented and easily distinguished. In the 1930s Peter Maurin, an
essayist, wrote, 'We need houses of hospitality to show what
idealism looks like when it's practised.'[6] The idealism he speaks
about is not an evangelical one, as he comes from the Irish
monastic tradition – indeed 'houses of hospitality' has that
monastic community feel to it – but he is highlighting the real
needs and desires of people.

Strangers, in the purist sense, are those who are dislocated;
that is to say, they are not connected to anyone who can give
security and fellowship. They may be detached from family or
church or country for a number of different reasons. The most
obvious examples are social or political refugees, and according
to Barbara Roche MP there is also a link between domestic violence and homelessness.[7] As soon as these people are welcomed
into our homes they are linked to a secure framework. When we
eat together we communicate with each other, with the possibility of resonating and connecting in new and exciting ways.

We all know testimonies of the transformation that takes
place when a person comes to know Jesus; it's that 'once you
were no people, but now you are God's people' scenario (1 Peter
2:10). These examples are not as common as we would like,
partly because 'church' is an alien place to many these days –
but to enter someone's home as an invited guest for a meal will
always be easier.

To open our home in this way requires an open heart, a listening ear and a mutual sharing of lives. The rewards and the enrich-

ing are well worth the demands. Hosts always experience blessing, for somehow they have been treading on holy ground (maybe
it's like having angels to stay). Matthew
25:31ff is an important text in this regard,
for the words 'I was hungry and you gave
me something to eat' (spoken by Jesus)
imply very plainly that guests at our table
in need of fellowship and food come in
the semblance of Jesus himself. If we bear
these breathtaking truths in mind when
we open our homes to others, we will
learn to look for the signs that Jesus has

*True hospitality
involves welcoming
others and
demonstrating love
to them for the
sheer joy of
doing so.*

begun to work in their lives. They may still be at the wooing stage,
or they may already be 'not far from the kingdom of God' (Mark
12:34); the fact is that if we are looking for such signs we will be
ready to serve God more fully in our hosting.

A relaxed environment

There is a lot more to hospitality than inviting friends to your
house for a meal or party. Even if you don't like entertaining,
you can serve others by exercising a hospitable attitude that will
extend God's love into any situation. True hospitality involves
welcoming others and demonstrating love to them for the sheer
joy of doing so, without expecting anything in return. It is to
build relationships with people in order that we may learn how
best to serve them. Taking the time to listen to others without
thinking of the next thing you want to say about yourself shows
that you care about them as individuals.

Be real. The Bible tells us that in our relationships with one
another we are to weep with those who weep and rejoice with
those who rejoice, so when you encounter someone who is
suffering, don't be afraid to cry with them if it comes naturally.
When you meet someone who is rejoicing, celebrate with them.
Always be willing to share the gospel with the people you are
serving as and when God brings about opportunities.

In our home, we have found that having easy-listening music playing quietly in the background helps people to relax. Soft lighting does the same. Seating is important too. Arrange the seating as much as possible in a circle, avoiding lines facing each other, and if you have a favourite seat don't make a beeline towards it before your guests are seated – if they choose your chair, tough! Seating that doesn't all face the TV demonstrates that relationships are more important. Other aspects of the room are important too. Try to make the room inviting; flowers and fruit are easy ways of doing this. Tables with interesting books or magazines around give an opportunity for people to browse naturally if you are preparing the meal or the phone goes.

Regarding the phone, leave it when you're in conversation with visitors – they must feel they are the most important people in your life at the moment. If the phone call is impor- tant, the person will leave a message, and if you don't have an answerphone or access to the 1571 service, you can can always dial 1471 to find out who called as soon as there's a lull. Mobile phones are worse intruders than land lines because we have them on our person. Put them away or switch them off.

If your visitors are staying over, provide clean towels and maybe place a vase of flowers or bowl of fruit in their room. A little time, thoughtfulness and effort will go a long way towards making people feel welcome.

Opening doors

Hospitality is all about opening doors to enter into a deeper and more meaningful relationship with each other. Opening the door is to allow another to share something of themselves. You are entering into their space; it's one of their 'personal rooms'. One way to open doors is to ask some questions, but these 'question doors' need to be used sparingly, lest your guest feels your hospitality is an inquisition rather than a useful launch into conversation. Listen to the answers and explore any common territory that you find in the 'room' that has been opened to you. Ask questions like: 'What's your reaction to this latest strike action in the news today?' or 'Why do you suppose things like this happen?'

Those who practise hospitality will find that their interest base broadens. It is impossible to practise hospitality if the topics of conversation have to revolve around your already established and narrow spheres of interest. I remember once talking to someone at a party who worked at Kew Gardens in the grasses section. What he didn't know about grasses was nobody's business; but actually that would be to coin an irrelevant phrase, because he thought it *was* everybody's business! If your pet subject is all you care about, the subject can become so boring that everyone will soon find imaginative ways to avoid entering into dialogue with you. The problem with conversations like this is that one person is trying to open a door, and the other is trying to squeeze their fellow conversant into the only open door in their personal space. In the case of my friend from Kew, interest was caught for a few minutes, because there are *some* interesting facts about grasses, but only fellow grass enthusiasts would stay interested for more than ten minutes.

Good relationships, from a conversation point of view, are those where both parties are aware of the interest-gauge of their companion, which for all but the extremely polite will be demonstrated in body language. So if in your conversation you haven't struck oil in the first few minutes, stop 'boring' and dig in another field – open another door.

Conversation is a true dialogue that is open to its own horizons and not congested by preconceived thoughts.

We hear a lot today about the death of conversation. This does not mean that no one talks any more; on the contrary, there's a great deal of talking going on. But talking is not the same as conversation. Conversation actually involves touching base with another person; it has to do with relationship. It is easy to talk to someone without entering into a genuine relationship with them.

People speak to each other for many reasons, and the straightforward communication of information is one of the primary uses of speech. Other uses include giving commands and making requests. Language is useful in these kinds of speaking. But why is conversation an art? I think it's because conversation is a true dialogue that is open to its own horizons and not congested by preconceived thoughts. It is a shared exploration of questions and theories. Idle chat and gossip is a way of merely spending time with someone and will become repetitious and ultimately boring. Conversation is an art because it takes practice and skill to draw out thought from talk; to share freely thoughts and emotions that will teach us something. Here are some pointers:

Shared experiences

A good conversation often starts with shared experiences. There is no replacement for the camaraderie that comes from mutual memories. For instance, if like many British people you have started a conversation based on the weather, you might say, 'Do you remember the storm of 1987?' A shared experience gives equal access and comparable knowledge to contribute to a conversation.

Paying attention to noteworthy events

Every day something happens that is worth remembering, and these occurrences can be used in conversation at a later date. The classic example of this is the terrorist attack on the World Trade Center in New York on 11th September 2001. It would be rare to find someone who hadn't watched this tragedy unfold without feeling the usual emotions of anger, sadness, fear and pain. These are emotions that can be shared, drawn out and shaped into a dialogue with Christian perspectives and therefore can be potentially life-changing. But in the process nothing has been forced, there has been no 'Bible-bashing', no dogma has been pontificated. Natural, common feelings have been pooled and painted onto a canvas that has brought clarity and perspective to a shared event.

Being vulnerable

It is not only the host who opens doors. Guests will also want to open a few of *your* doors. It is surprising how many are comfortable exploring the personal territory of others, yet cower when the tables are turned. Being vulnerable, laying yourself open to scrutiny, is not comfortable, at least to begin with, yet it's a necessary exercise if we are serious about building relationships. It all comes down to self-image in the final analysis. If we are unhappy about who we are, what we look like and what we do, we will run away from any situation that requires vulnerability.

Some people will tend to wait for others to take the first step: it may be that they are waiting for attention to be given to them, so that in a small way the love or friendship being shown counters their initial vulnerability and it becomes 'safe' to proceed. Others are too shy to take the first step because of a fear that they will be rejected. They build personas that give the message, 'I don't need you. I am very self-sufficient.'

However, it doesn't take long to discover that putting on a persona is like living behind a transparent wall, and it is very lonely. You can see people in the room, you can even want to communicate with them, yet you somehow remain separated from them, and (just as frustrating) they also see you but find it difficult to connect with you because they read your nervous body language.

In fact, these walls have a way of highlighting all the negatives. The world becomes a frightening place on the other side. Yet what is seen through the wall is the reflection of what you have been projecting. Perhaps what people see on your side of the wall is a person who seems aloof and not very friendly, so it becomes a vicious circle that is often hard to break.

For years I suffered from a fear of entering a room full of

people I didn't know. This became a big issue when God called me to the pastoral ministry! I had to teach myself that God's calling on my life involved the need for me to break the ice in conversing, and therefore God would enable me to do it. I had to learn that being vulnerable was not the same as being afraid; that the former was not a bad thing, and it was the latter (the fear) that I had to defeat. It took a couple of years of struggling, but I did it.

Learning to be vulnerable is to learn that it's perfectly OK to show our feelings without knowing what the response will be. It is a peeling away of the wrappers. There will be times when the fear of being thought a fool returns, but it's possible to push on through. Someone once said that love is spelt 'RISK' and that suggests high vulnerability. But it's worth it.

If we let others into our 'life rooms' it will enable us to experience authentic, supportive relationships.

So what does being vulnerable actually mean? It means that there will be times when we have to face emotional pain because something that had been said to us had triggered a response to an event deep down in our subconscious. It means that sometimes people will take advantage of us, or abuse our friendship. Sometimes it will mean feeling ensnared or locked up in a situation where our feelings and rights are ignored.

Perhaps one of the most fear-provoking aspects of allowing ourselves to be vulnerable is to be at the point in a relationship where we feel we can probably safely and freely speak of our innermost feelings and fears to another but we are afraid of the possibility they might use such confidences against us. King David spoke of a situation where his closest companion turned on him and used information shared in private to try to bring about his downfall (Psalm 55:12–15).

Many avoid this road because of basic survival instincts – an insecurity and lack of self-confidence coupled with a lack of trust in others and even themselves. Such people often demonstrate an overwhelming need for personal privacy and confidentiality. There may be a fear of the unknown and a deep-rooted inability to forget past hurts, injustices and pain – something that would actually bring 'closure' and forgiveness.

If we let others into our 'life rooms' it will enable us to experience authentic, supportive relationships and will give us a healthy perspective of our situation with its problems and concerns. It will help us to be open to change, scrutinising our behaviour patterns in a positive way, which in turn will give us the opportunity to rid ourselves of unproductive habits that impede our emotional health and personal growth. So despite the risks it's encouraging to open ourselves to the possibility of growing emotionally and spiritually by a willingness to take chances and try new experiences and challenges as we seek to build relationships.

As always, our best example is Jesus. On the day that we now call Palm Sunday, people waved palms, as they would for any victor, as Jesus rode into Jerusalem on a donkey. People had welcomed Alexander the Great 300 years earlier in this way. It is true that Jesus (the King of kings) has the victory, but it is not as simple as that. He was, at that point, victorious, but not in the way people expected. Unlike Alexander the Great, he was not victorious by forcing his enemies to yield. No, his victory was in his vulnerability.

It is only when we are willing to expose our true selves that we are able to really touch base with others.

To recognise that vulnerability in Jesus is to begin to understand our own vulnerability. Take a close look at how he was obedient to God's will, allowing the events of his capture, torture, humiliation and final crucifixion to unfold. He was no coward, no political martyr – just absolutely confident in the faultlessness of God's plan, assured of who he was and what was being accomplished. This inspires us to learn how to stand tall in who we are by God's grace. It is to know Jesus and to be known by Jesus.

It is there, on the cross, that God meets with us at the point of our own human vulnerability. And it is there that we can deal with every notion that would stop us being vulnerable, and ultimately stop us from being real with ourselves about ourselves. It is only when we are willing to expose our true selves that we are able to really touch base with others and begin to build lasting relationships.

Looking for ways to bless

As relationships develop, needs become known and therefore opportunities to bless become apparent. It is not rocket science to be able to see a need and seek to meet it, yet how often do we refuse to get involved and retreat into our castles? It is one of those twenty-first-century Western blights on our society that we pursue a policy of non-involvement. Everything militates against us getting involved, as if our British reserve needed the additional problems of apathy and a fear of failing to be politically correct.

To illustrate this, Alexander Kinglake records meeting some fellow travellers in the middle of the Syrian desert in 1835. As Kinglake looked over the bare isolation of the desert, three other camels appeared on the horizon. As they drew nearer, it became easier to identify what sort of travellers these may be. Kinglake observed an English shooting jacket and European features:

'As we approached each other, it became with me a question whether we should speak. I thought it likely that the stranger would accost me, and in the event of his doing so, I was quite ready to be as sociable and chatty as I could according to my nature . . .' As it happened the leader of this party was an English army officer heading home from India. They met in the middle of nowhere, no one else about and they raised their caps to one another: 'we passed . . . as distantly as if we had passed in Pall Mall. Not a word was said.'[8]

In the past few years we have also had to contend with the fact that it is wise for us to be careful that any contact with the opposite sex or young children is not misconstrued. It's another risk factor, but how easily are we prepared to give up the call of Jesus to help those in need? We have to find ways to fulfil our calling to the most vulnerable in our society without ignoring new policies of political correctness. It is so easy to hide behind state help, our lack of time or our inability to really understand the need. There is never any shortage of excuses at our disposal. Sadly, they all point to our selfish desires that tell us to remain aloof from the needs of others.

We have to start thinking outwards. When we go to the shops, might there be some way we can bless a neighbour by getting something for them while we're there? When we cook the Sunday roast, might there be someone we can bless by inviting them to share it with us? When we drive to church, might there be someone we can bless with a lift? When someone has shared a need with us, might we show our compassion by offering to pray with them there and then? When we observe an accident, or the aftermath of one, might we not take time to ensure the necessary emergency services have been called and wait until they arrive? It's all Good Samaritan stuff, and that is not to say it puts our names in lights – it's the command of our Saviour to do it without thinking about the cost or repercussions.

Hospitable homes

Hospitality is costly, both on your privacy and on the purse, but it's a way of giving to God. Let me give you a very bad example of hospitality. When I was a student I travelled from Surrey to Scotland with a friend to visit some friends of my parents who had often been guests in our family home at weekends and Christmas. We had a superb time with them; their generosity seemed endless as they showed us around the locality and suggested the best places to see. Unfortunately, this superb hospitality was ruined when on the last day we presented them with some flowers and groceries for looking after us so well and they presented us with an itemised bill for everything we had used, including electricity, food and water! Our host was a lecturer in economics and he was deadly serious. But to give with one hand and take with the other is not the hospitality of the Scriptures. Our homes and our hearts are to be totally open towards our guests.

That example is an extreme and, I hope, rare one. Many enjoy opening their homes to friends and are sacrificial in doing so. It's that fact that I want to build upon.

Single

You don't need to be married or have a family to have a hospitable home or a ministry in hospitality. The number of single adults in society and in our churches is growing: 48 per cent of adults over 16 were single in 2001. They may be single people who will be married later, or single by choice because God in his wisdom has wanted it that way, or single having once been married, or single through bereavement. Whatever the reason, the ministry of single people, often overlooked by the church and sometimes by the people themselves, can be of huge significance in the community. It is important that single people become aware of their significance and purpose in Christ.

Paul said that, in his opinion, singleness allows undistracted devotion to the Lord in ways that married people cannot match (1 Corinthians 7:32–36). Indeed, our faith rests on Jesus, a single man from Galilee, whose ministry was preceded by a single man named John the Baptist, and whose early church mission beyond Israel's borders was first modelled by a single person named Paul. So single Christians are instrumental to God's purpose, not because they are on their own, but because they are Christians who are crucial players in enabling the truth of Jesus to be shared in the community.

The other side of the 'single' coin is that they have a need to be incorporated into the life and fellowship of the Christian community. Ever since the time when Adam experienced loneliness without another to complement and share his humanity, many have identified with his feelings. Paul visualised the church as an oasis where all people are valued and every gift is appreciated – a place where all can find fellowship and support. All who belong to Christ are 'Abraham's seed, and heirs according to the promise' (Galatians 3:29). When we think of hospitality, we must include in our thinking those singles who may be lonely, or have other needs simply because they are on their own. In 1999, 22 per cent of all families were headed by a single parent, as compared to just 7 per cent 25 years earlier. That is why the needs of this rapidly growing social group in our society must be recognised and cared for by the church. The first organised meeting of the early church (Acts 6) was in response to the needs of single adults (widows). Both Old and New Testaments demand special care for widows and orphans (Exodus 22:22; 1 Timothy 5:3) and the Lord is clearly on the side of those who are alone (Deuteronomy 10:18; Psalm 146:9).

Married

God made marriage, and in marriage a husband and wife (and later children also) are a team. Priscilla and Aquila are the only couple mentioned in any detail in the New Testament, and they are a good example of a team who served God together. They were tentmakers in Corinth and that was Paul's adopted trade during his travels, so this was probably how they met. Paul was invited to their home as a guest and stayed for a year and a half.

Their relationship during that time obviously grew and deepened, for Paul asked Priscilla and Aquila to accompany him when he continued his missionary journey to Ephesus. After preaching in the synagogue there, Paul left Priscilla and Aquila in Ephesus to continue the work. This fact shows that Paul knew them well enough to entrust the preaching and teaching to them. They must have ministered successfully there about the Messiah, because in Acts 18:27 we are told that by the time Apollos got there, others had become Christians. And later in 1 Corinthians 16:19, Paul writes a letter to Corinth from Ephesus, stating that the Ephesian church meets in Priscilla and Aquila's house.

When Apollos came to Ephesus, he began to speak boldly in the synagogue. When Priscilla and Aquila heard him, they invited him to their home and explained to him the way of God 'more adequately' (Acts 18:24–26). I would like to have sat in on that conversation. Here was a respected preacher who taught about Jesus accurately enough, but Priscilla and Aquila recognised that the fire of the Holy Spirit was missing. So what did they do? They used their home and the harmony of their marriage relationship to demonstrate God's love and over dinner they shared what they had discovered about the baptism of the Holy Spirit.

Exercising the gift of hospitality is one of the most rewarding things you will ever do.

Offering hospitality to ministers and leaders is an important ministry. For those in full-time Christian work, whether at home or in mission abroad, there is a unique loneliness. Many people are known, but few friendships are formed. Full-time workers not only need the prayers of their flock but value immensely being prayed *with* by the flock and being shown practical gratitude for their work.

Priscilla and Aquila were ready for God to use them anytime, anywhere. They worked together in ministry, bringing people to the Lord, opening their home whenever needed, giving of themselves to people who needed discipling, and letting go of their disciples when their work with them was done. This was indeed a couple God could count on. Is your home and your marriage open for him to use? Ministering together in your home by exercising the gift of hospitality is one of the most rewarding things you will ever do.

Putting things right

I heard of the following incident recently that illustrates an inspired act of hospitality. It was told me by some friends who came to lunch, and concerns a friend of theirs (we'll call him Gerry). Gerry was involved in a car accident in the

Birmingham area. It was his fault and the innocent party in the incident was an Indian gentleman (we'll call him Raj). Both Gerry and Raj went through the normal procedures for this kind of incident with the police and the insurance brokers. When it was all over, Raj rang Gerry and invited him for a meal. The explanation Raj gave was that they had carried out all the legal requirements properly and completely by the book, but it was now necessary to make sure that the relationship between them, should they ever meet again, was also right and that there was no bitterness or hostility. The meal would be the occasion to bury the incident and ensure they were on good terms. Gerry left that meal amazed. Amazed that there was such an outcome to what was obviously a difficult event, but amazed and saddened that it was Raj, the innocent party, who had taken the initiative to restore proper relational harmony and not Gerry, who caused the accident.

This incident highlights the everyday opportunities we all face for healing relationships through the medium of hospitality, even in situations where legally and socially a calamity has been properly dealt with. It graphically reveals that deeper relationships with our neighbours are not only possible but, from an emotional point of view, far more valuable than a simple nod of recognition or a range of avoidance tactics.

The incident also opens up the often tricky but very important principle of repentance and forgiveness that is one of the foundational bricks for building good relationships. The twin values of repentance and forgiveness can often be shown around the meal table in our homes as we practise hospitality. In Matthew 18 Jesus talks about a biblical grievance procedure. It is a three-stage procedure and the entire purpose is to bring reconciliation between two parties who are in disagreement. The starting point is the most interesting in the context of Christian behaviour today. We are to start by trying to sort out the grievance between ourselves, and if that fails the second stage is to bring in an umpire. This person isn't there to support either party's point of view, but to see that there is fair play and reasonable behaviour. Both parties might have an umpire. The third stage is to take the grievance to the church.

In the first stage, only two people know what the grievance is all about. In the second stage only a maximum of four people know. In the third stage many people know about it. These days, unfortunately, too many grievances are heard by too many ears, and these are often ears that should not hear. Sometimes when the grievance is about something that was said, others hear about it before the other party is aware that they have caused a problem at all!

I am convinced that Jesus expected most grievances to be solved at the first stage, when only the two involved know about it and no one else need ever know. Imagine how much better that would be: no one to hear gossip that distorts a person's character; no resolved hurts brought up in a different context later on; no avoiding certain people under the pretext that they've harmed you or your friend. And how wonderful to sort this out in the privacy of your home around the mutually enjoyable necessity of eating together.

Failing to follow this pattern is very damaging indeed. After teaching about the three stages, Jesus continues with these words: 'I tell you the truth, whatever you bind on earth will be bound in heaven, and whatever you loose on earth will be loosed in heaven.' In the context, Jesus is saying that our adherence to, or our disregard of, this teaching either binds people up or releases them. Forgiveness brings reconciliation, reconciliation brings agreement and agreement brings liberty. Peter, like many down through the ages, didn't really understand that, so he asked a question indicating his inner thoughts about his right to refuse to forgive: 'Lord, how many times shall I forgive my brother when he sins against me? Up to seven times?' (Matthew 18:21).

To be fair to Peter, the rabbis taught that you only need to forgive three times. Rabbi Jose Ben Hanina taught that anyone who begs forgiveness from his neighbour must not do so more than three times. Another rabbi, Jose Ben Jehuda, taught that if a man commits an offence once, then he is to be forgiven. If he commits an offence a second and third time, he can also be forgiven. But on the fourth time he should not be forgiven.

Jesus' answer reveals once again the nature and heart of God. His arms are open wide; there is no restriction on whom he touches, accepts or forgives. Indeed he has a limitless capacity for forgiveness. So it is no surprise that Jesus should say, 'I tell you, not seven times, but seventy-seven times' (Matthew 18:22). There is no limit.

We are not placed on earth to judge people or condemn one another. That is God's business. Our task is to forgive, and go on forgiving, even our worst enemies, and leave the judging to the God of mercy and justice. Forgiveness should be a way of life for the Christian and we should not act as if we are keeping a notebook adding up merits and failures. The notion that implies 'that's it, you've gone too far now' should, says Jesus, never be found in our lives. Paul tells the Corinthian church that among other things love 'keeps no record of wrongs' (1 Corinthians 13:5). If we live a forgiving life we will never concern ourselves with limits, because forgiveness is as limitless as life itself.

Allow me to commend to you the practice of hospitality to those with whom you have a grievance or where relational distance for some reason or other has been allowed to increase.

PUTTING PRINCIPLES INTO PRACTICE

1. Describe some of the emotions you feel when it is time to come home again after being away.
2. 'Home expresses one of the most fundamental social, economic, political and personal realities of the ancient world.' Make a list of the most common realities under the three headings within this quote.
3. Read Acts 2:46. Have you ever broken bread with other Christians in your home? If you have, describe the aspects of that meal which you tried to re-create from how you

imagined the Last Supper to have been. Why do you think Christians don't generally practise breaking bread in homes as in New Testament times?

4. Give the reasons for the current trend to eat meals while watching TV. Would it be possible for you to ensure at least two meals a week became a family time around the table?

5. Discuss who you think are the vulnerable in your neighbourhood and why. What measures could you, or your group, take to give hospitality to them?

4

Prioritising Relationships

'When you give a luncheon or dinner, do not invite your
friends, your brothers or relatives, or your rich neighbours
. . . But when you give a banquet, invite the poor, the crippled, the lame, the blind, and you will be blessed.' (Luke
14:12–14)

According to need

It is Saturday, the Jewish Sabbath, and Jesus, having already
been the guest of tax collectors and friends, is now invited to
dinner by an influential Pharisee, 'a prominent Pharisee' (Luke
14:1), the most zealous of all law-keepers among the Jews.
Since this was the Sabbath, all the food would have been
prepared ahead of time for this rather large dinner party.
Lighting or keeping alight a fire for cooking wasn't allowed on
the Sabbath itself (which began at sunset Friday night), so food
was prepared on Friday. There were normally three meals
regarded as Sabbath meals: Friday evening, Saturday morning,
and a light meal following the time of Saturday afternoon
prayer. We're not told which meal Jesus was invited to, but the
Friday evening meal would have been the most elaborate of the
three.

This particular Pharisee seems to have had an ulterior motive
for inviting one of his guests. Jesus was invited to see how he
might react to their interpretation of the law. The Greek word
describing their intentions is *paratereo*, which means 'watch
closely' or 'observe carefully'. From the context this can take on
the meaning 'watch maliciously' or even 'lie in wait for',

because they were clearly trying to trip Jesus up – it seems they wanted to catch him breaking the Sabbath law.

There was a man at the meal table who was afflicted with dropsy (Greek *hydropikos*). Dropsy, or oedema as it is known today, is an abnormal accumulation of fluid in the body cavities and tissues. Often there is puffiness in the face and swelling of the legs. It isn't so much a disease as a sign of an underlying cause, such as congestive heart failure, liver disease or kidney disease. One wonders if this man was deliberately planted to catch Jesus out; we certainly ought to question why the Pharisees had invited a diseased man at all, since the Pharisees, of all people, were obsessive about ritual cleanness, and a diseased man might render them unclean. On the other hand, it is not recorded that Jesus picked up on this particular act of hypocrisy. Perhaps the man was a wealthy Pharisee himself. He may not at this stage have had any signs or symptoms that rendered him ceremonially unclean, but he was in obvious poor health.

Now, as it happened, this man was seated right in front of (*emprosthen*) Jesus, where his health couldn't go unnoticed and would therefore immediately draw Jesus to desire to heal him. The Pharisees would have watched Jesus closely. Would he, first of all, wash his hands in the traditional ritual fashion? Would he break any of their laws? Jesus didn't immediately heal the man. Instead, he asked a question that might cause them to give him permission to do so: ' "Is it lawful to heal on the Sabbath or not?" But they remained silent' (Luke 14:3–4). They could have answered, outlining what was or wasn't allowed on the Sabbath. To bandage a wound to keep it from getting worse was allowed, but any treatment to improve a wound or heal a sickness was definitely forbidden unless considered life-threatening. Actually, Mosaic law (the law given by Moses) didn't prohibit healing on the Sabbath; it was only rabbinical tradition, after years of clarification as to what the law allowed. The silence of the host and his friends to the question Jesus posed meant that no one could easily accuse Jesus of breaking the law if he went ahead and administered healing.

There was something else that Jesus wanted to address here; it appears that the Pharisees' agenda at this dinner was primarily selfish.

> When he noticed how the guests picked the places of honour at the table, he told them this parable: 'When someone invites you to a wedding feast, do not take the place of honour, for a person more distinguished than you may have been invited. If so, the host who invited both of you will come and say to you, "Give this man your seat." Then, humiliated, you will have to take the least important place.' (Luke 14:7–9)

Just as the disciples had argued at the last Passover meal about who was the greatest, here also there was a clear pecking order among these invited guests. Sometimes at special meals we have guest cards to indicate where the guests should sit, but there was of course nothing like this, so as a guest entered he would look for the place where he would be honoured or where he could carry out the most effective 'networking'. The nearer the host you sat, the greater status you had. Jesus wanted to show that such a social tradition had no place in the kingdom of God. You will remember that James and John had a mother who tried to ensure that at the last day her two sons would take the preferred places at the banquet table, one on his right and the other on his left (Matthew 20:21–23). Jesus left this mother in no doubt that this was not a suitable request.

Although the guests may have tried to engineer the best place for themselves, it was really up to the host to seat, or reseat, his guests where he wanted them to be. Jesus gave a rather humorous example of the host asking an overconfident guest to give up his place of honour to another guest. The result was that the embarrassed guest was relegated to the only seat left at the table, the least important place. The one who had sought to advance his social standing ended up being publicly humiliated.

Jesus used this example to teach a kingdom principle:

'But when you are invited, take the lowest place, so that when your host comes, he will say to you, "Friend, move up to a better place." Then you will be honoured in the presence of all your fellow guests. For everyone who exalts himself will be humbled, and he who humbles himself will be exalted.' (Luke 14:10–11)

Of course, Jesus is indicating here that it is not just a dinner host who might humble you. He is also implying that if we have this attitude that drives us to find the exalted place at a dinner table, the same attitude is very likely to be present in all aspects of our lives and then it will be God himself who humbles us. It is more prudent to be humble before God and then God can exalt us.

Imagine the scene at this dinner. In our culture we would have said that a host who spoke as bluntly as this was exceedingly rude. In Jesus' culture, however, it wasn't seen in the same way.

Jesus is therefore teaching us to invite those who are least able to reciprocate.

For one thing Jesus was recognised as a rabbi (because he had disciples) and the culture allowed rabbis to take every opportunity to express their views on lifestyle and tradition. What is always different about Jesus is the way he uses the Scriptures they know so well in a totally different way from every other rabbi. Many remarked through his short ministry period that no one taught like this man (Matthew 13:54).

Jesus continued throughout the dinner to talk about motives. He addressed the host and his motives.

'When you give a luncheon or dinner, do not invite your friends, your brothers or relatives, or your rich neighbours; if you do, they may invite you back and so you will be repaid. But when you give a banquet, invite the poor, the crippled, the lame, the blind, and you will be blessed. Although they cannot repay you, you will be repaid at the resurrection of the righteous.' (Luke 14:12–14)

Jesus is therefore teaching us to invite those who are least able to reciprocate. Our motivation for the invitations we give should be genuine love and the goodness of our heart. It is to be a kingdom of God custom to invite the poor and the needy, the ones who don't often get invited out. This ensures we don't look for status or earthly reward. Then God will reward us.

Now, there is no better cover for truth than a half-truth. The half-truth here indicates that Jesus intends by this teaching to end all family meals and gatherings of friends. But the full truth is that there is, in every human heart, a tendency to live by the law of reciprocation. There is a subtle inclination in our flesh to do what will make life as comfortable as possible and to avoid what will inconvenience us or upset our peaceful lives. So we are not naturally inclined to ask into our homes those who will take up our time or be a burden to us, or those who could become a problem for life. Part of hosting in a comfortable and pleasant way is to anticipate that our invitations will be matched one day and we will be hosted by those who are now our guests. This wrong attitude is so opposed to the kingdom of God that Jesus tells a parable about it:

> 'There was a rich man who was dressed in purple and fine linen and lived in luxury every day. At his gate was laid a beggar named Lazarus, covered with sores and longing to eat what fell from the rich man's table. Even the dogs came and licked his sores. The time came when the beggar died and the angels carried him to Abraham's side. The rich man also died and was buried. In hell, where he was in torment, he looked up and saw Abraham far away, with Lazarus by his side. So he called to him, "Father Abraham, have pity on me and send Lazarus to dip the tip of his finger in water and cool my tongue, because I am in agony in this fire." But Abraham said, "Son, remember that in your lifetime you received your good things, while Lazarus received bad things, but now he is comforted here and you are in agony."' (Luke 16:19–25)

According to Jewish culture, a banquet was a symbol of the future and eternal reign of God. The Jews saw the coming time of a new heaven and earth as the hosting of a banquet by the Messiah. So the parable of the banquet is, in fact, concerned with teachings on the salvation that the future reign of God brings.

Through this parable, and others like it, Jesus shows the preference of priority to the poor over the rich in this reign of God.

Why didn't the rich man give Lazarus the crumbs from his table? Because Lazarus was in no position to repay. Clearly the law of reciprocation governed the rich man's life. He wore the finest clothes and feasted sumptuously, but he did not bother himself with the poor or even the sick man at his very door.

If as a result of the teaching of Scripture we are to adopt a different attitude to hospitality – one that gives preference to those who are unlikely to repay – we must consider who would come into this category in the society in which we live today. If I can take a phrase of Jesus out of context, he said that the poor would always be with us, and therefore our consideration to reform our attitudes should start here. But who are the poor?

Many will immediately think of the homeless at this point, so that's a good place to start. Apart from legal definitions of homelessness, a broad definition would be either those who are literally without a roof over their heads or those who are compelled to live in overcrowded, dangerous, illegal or very temporary accommodation, such as bed and breakfast hotels, hostels, a friend's or relative's floor or squats.

Homelessness has increased significantly in recent years due to a number of economic and social factors, including the decline of availability in rented accommodation, lack of affordable accommodation for those on low incomes, rising unemployment, domestic violence and the growth in single households (although recent government initiatives have reduced the number of rough sleepers).

Perhaps the most disturbing statistics about homelessness in the United Kingdom are those that show the number of young children involved. According to one television newscaster covering the Millie Dowler case, one in nine children under 16 runs away each year: a total of 100,000 children each year, and seven per cent of them are under eight, one in seven being sexually or physically assaulted.

Such statistics dramatically gnaw away at the Christian conscience, reminding us that as a church and as individuals we have a responsibility to provide for people in need when they cross our paths. But more than that, Christians have a responsibility to support charities and organisations that are proactive in alleviating the situation.

When Jesus said that he was giving us a new commandment, not only to love God with all our heart, soul and mind but also to 'love one another as I have loved you' (John 13:34), he was laying down his expectation that his followers would stand apart from the social agendas of each age to reach out unconditionally to such needy people. When he added that 'by this all men will know that you are my disciples, if you love one another', he was saying that by reaching out to the poor and needy we would educate the neighbourhood as to exactly what true Christian discipleship involved.

Learning curves

Discipleship has become a new maxim in evangelical circles. Despite the good basic Christianity courses like Alpha and the Y course, there is still a need for discipleship. It is one thing to teach people about the faith and quite another to train them to live it. In fact teaching about discipleship has limited value, for discipleship is learned by observation in tandem with teaching. No one these days really has time to train disciples as Jesus did, but there are certain principles we could adopt. The Greek word for discipleship means 'exact following'. The method of discipleship that Jesus used could be described as reproduction through observation. If as believers and followers of Jesus we live in such a way as to imitate Christ so closely, so exactly, allowing others to observe how we act and react in all kinds of situations, then we will produce disciples. Clearly those of us who are parents have a primary responsibility to do this within the family. Every child observes and learns ways of being and living from their parents, and it is sometimes so exact that it can be embarrassing!

How can this learning by observation work in the wider family and in the community? It can only happen as we openly, but normally and naturally, live out our Christian life wherever we are. We will reproduce a family of believers that know the way and the life because they have seen it in us. It will mean that we take the time to 'father' and 'mother' young believers and desire to see them established. Paul wanted to see more father figures in the church. Why? Because they are key to healthy discipleship. Sometimes we are so busy that we don't stop to think that in the

> *We will reproduce a family of believers that know the way and the life because they have seen it in us.*

things that make us busy we could have an apprentice or two. Take a young Christian under your wing when you do a task in the church, prayerwalk in the community, help a neighbour, invite a non-Christian for a meal, work with the needy, prepare a talk, and so on. Apprenticeship is an old practice that would be well worth resurrecting in our churches.

Let's face it: none of us is indispensable, however successful we are in what we do, it is of restricted value if we leave a gaping hole when we go. Somebody once said that success without a successor is failure. The other word to describe this activity that has become popular in recent years is the word 'mentoring'. It is a word that comes from Greek mythology. Mentor was Homer's wise and dependable friend in his 'Odyssey'. Ulysses employed him as the teacher and guardian of his son while he was fighting in the Trojan wars. John Mallison defines the mentoring process that we know today as 'a dynamic, intentional relationship of trust in which one person enables another to maximise the grace of God in their life and service'.[1] It is the process that we see in Jesus' statement to Peter that after his own trials he was to put what he had learned to good use by helping fellow disciples to become stronger (Luke 22:32).

This kind of mentoring or discipleship was part of everyday life in the Old Testament: examples such as Jethro and Moses, Moses and Joshua, David and Jonathan stand out. In the New

Testament, apart from the exemplary pattern of Jesus with the twelve disciples, Barnabas and Paul, Priscilla and Aquila with Apollos, and Paul and Timothy are all good examples. In John Wesley's specific writings for his followers he says, 'Watch over one another in love.'[2] It could be argued that this was the building block not only for his class meetings but for all successful house groups since.

So let me encourage you to find ways of reproducing in others what is godly in you. 'Making disciples' (Matthew 28:20) can sound pretty pushy, but the original has the sense of enabling rather than enforcing. Jesus, when he called his disciples around him, proclaimed that they had been witnesses of all they had seen (Luke 24:48). A witness is simply one who has observed something happen. It's not second- or third-hand information; it's personal experience that needs to be passed on.

I believe that as we follow in this way there is more opportunity for others to observe that 'by this all men will know that you are my disciples, if you love one another' (John 13:34). A difference between Christians and non-Christians is bound to be evident, for the values, behaviour and attitudes that are all around us today are based on anti-Christian principles, where there are no absolutes, no unshakeable universal truth. The normal Christian boundaries inspired by the Ten Commandments are eroding; everyone has become their own judge and negotiator for what is right and wrong, and traditional authority figures are rejected and not honoured. But it's not all bad news. The same state of affairs has made many despair and search for answers elsewhere. Society's infrastructures are not working as they should because of it, the great god of technology has not answered or solved world issues, and those who say they love but act as if they don't care are seen for what they are.

The last surviving disciple of Jesus, John, wrote in his first epistle:

This is how we know what love is: Jesus Christ laid down his life for us. And we ought to lay down our lives for our brothers. If anyone has material possessions and sees his brother in need but has no pity on him, how can the love of God be in him? Dear children, let us not love with words or tongue but with actions and in truth. (1 John 3:16–18)

These people mentioned by John could be described as the obvious homeless. But society is also full of people with another kind of homelessness: they may well be described as the relationally homeless. Just as the physically homeless tend to drift, so do those who are relationally homeless. They don't stay long enough in any relationships to begin to really get to know others or to be known by those who would like to befriend them. Their drifting patterns cause them to miss out on both receiving and giving love.

Most friendships entail varying degrees of mentoring or discipleship that are very informal. Being aware of the dynamics of discipleship will often lead us deeper into a relationship that becomes more effective in producing support, encouragement and change. Offering hospitality again and again to those who find it hard to make lasting and deep relationships is a long-term grind and will involve systematic teaching to correct their self-assessment and the value they place on their lives. But eventually some will respond and it will be a rewarding ministry.

Missing out

There are many other groups that also miss out on the normal offers of hospitality among Christians, because they represent a difficulty to us or they complicate the hospitality norms in some way. These include single-parent families and large families. The former are often neglected because potential hosts feel that single parents will become dependants looking for a degree of counselling or advice that they cannot give. The latter are often neglected simply because a family of five or six is a big addition to most households. One family of six said to us when we invited them round for lunch that they hadn't been invited out as a family for several years. That's sad. To invite such a family may be a larger undertaking than you're normally used to, but you would be more of a blessing to the recipients than you could conceive.

Special needs

Another group that often miss out on hospitality are families who have children with special needs. Again, potential hosts fear that they will not be able to cope well with any awkward or embarrassing incidents, and that somehow it will ruin any relationship that currently exists. This is a groundless fear because such families are well aware of potential difficulties and know how to set hosts at ease. It is always sensible to prepare for such a visit by asking the parents if there are things that they need to be aware of when a special needs child comes into a new environment. This gives the parent the opportunity, perhaps for the first time with the potential host, to explain exactly what the nature of the needs are. Knowledge often drives fears and apprehensions away.

The elderly

Many elderly people are invited out by other elderly people, but I know that many long to be invited out by younger folk, whether single or in families. This is a particular blessing when grandparents have died, because the elderly in the community can often play that role for young children. A house group can often organise events in nursing homes for the elderly, a monthly Sunday afternoon service or a Christmas carol concert. These can be accompanied with food provided by the group.

Missionaries

Another group that need relationship and hospitality are missionaries. We often speak of the cultural shock that missionaries face if they are ministering in a culture that is very different from their own. In fact, for many the culture shock is on returning home for a break. True it has taken time to build relationships with others in a new culture, but imagine returning home to find that the church leadership has changed, friends have moved on, or the way things are done has changed. Then imagine facing a supermarket again after three or four years in a developing country where, if you can get the food, there certainly isn't a choice. Suddenly you have to make choices about insignificant things like cereals and teas. Missionaries returning home for a break can therefore feel disorientated all over again. What they need is hospitality and help to make them feel at home again.

Leadership

Finally, church leaders shouldn't be neglected from those you wish to give hospitality to. Mostly we have enjoyed good hospitality in the pastorate, but in one church we pastored we spent the first five weeks in someone else's house. This situation was an act of hospitality in itself; the single lady who owned the house went to live with a friend so that we could have the use of her home. The sad accompaniment to this lovely story is that only one family in the fellowship invited us for a meal during this time when we were not in our own house, and they were already friends of 15 years' standing. A new pastor and family always find that the best way to get to know their flock is in their own homes over a meal.

> *To be in leadership is often a lonely place to be.*

To be in leadership is often a lonely place to be. When we were youth pastors, and later, when I was an assistant pastor, we had plenty of meals with other members of the fellowship, but when I became senior pastor in the same church, there was a noticeable reduction. I don't know whether people were afraid of saying the wrong thing, or whether they believed I wouldn't be capable of talking about anything other than church issues, but it was not pleasant. In fact, someone once said to me that they didn't want to be seen as one of the pastor's 'favourites' so they wouldn't be inviting us round for a meal. It's an attitude that reveals again the Western view that hospitality is only given so that something can be gained. Imagine what Jesus' reaction would have been if Martha, Mary and Lazarus had said that to him!

Needy times

There are special times in the year when the needy are most vulnerable. Christmas is an obvious time to watch out for any in the church or in your neighbourhood who are 'home alone'. But there are other times too. If you know someone who has been ill or in hospital, offering a place to recuperate is a lovely ministry. I remember after I had had an operation on my back, a friend rang and asked whether the family would benefit from a few days away from the hurly-burly of our manse life. If we have houses that can accommodate others in this way it is a godly use of God-given resources to open up our homes for such ministry. If we don't have a big place, a meal and part of the day together is just as valid. Holiday time can be a very difficult time for the lonely and those in single-parent families or large families who cannot afford to go away.

Most have seen the Mr Bean sketch when he goes alone to a restaurant on his birthday. Having written a card to himself, he opens it and reacts suitably surprised as he reads what he wrote. We can laugh at this, but it is a fact that for some people birthdays are sad, lonely times. It is a good idea to try and find out the birthday dates of those who might fall into this category. It is also a good practice to remember the anniversary of loved ones who have died. On a practical note, this sort of information can be shared with the relevant local house group so that a card may be sent or a visit made from Christians in the area.

PUTTING PRINCIPLES INTO PRACTICE

1. 'Dear children, let us not love with words or tongue but with actions and in truth' (1 John 3:18). Do you think your local churches are meeting the felt needs of your community?

What actions could you, as an individual, take to fulfil this scripture?

2. How has God blessed you? (Think about your family, abilities, resources, training, privileged experiences, etc.)

3. Who are the people who really listen to you? How does that make you feel about them and about yourself? How do you feel about people who don't listen to you?

4. List the contacts you have among the elderly, the young, families with special needs, self-help groups and special needs groups. Is there a Christian presence there? Could you be part of the support or team? Could your home be used in any way for this work?

5. Discuss the possible reasons that Mary, Martha and Lazarus had to make their home available to Jesus. Why didn't more families do this? Bearing in mind the view held by Jesus' own family about him (Mark 3:21), were there any risks involved for this family to be so hospitable? Can you identify any similar issues for us today?

6. Itemise a few things that you do in the church, home or community where you could have an apprentice.

5

Friendship Evangelism

To the weak I became weak, to win the weak. I have become all things to all men so that by all possible means I might save some.

(1 Corinthians 9:22)

The nature of friendship evangelism

The idea of friendship evangelism sounds inspired, but the cynic in me rather naughtily wonders if there is ever any mileage in evangelism that is devoid of friendship. Then I wonder why the phrase caught on so readily as the adage of those who have a heart for evangelism. But despite that, the phrase clearly describes what evangelism should be about. It is less about 'saving souls' and everything to do with saving people. The word 'soul' seems to stop strangely short of relationship, and relationships with non-Christians are what we should be praying for.

My early Christian years were spent in an environment where the Christians around me prayed in meetings for the salvation of souls. I have often felt that such people missed something of Jesus' practice of ministering to the whole person. Praying for souls to be saved in a gospel meeting seems to encourage the idea that we're just concerned with 'pegging up' another name on a heavenly (or earthly) chart. It requires nothing more than being faithful to the gospel message. Praying that we might befriend non-Christians in order to seek an opportunity to share the gospel with them will, by definition, involve time, sensitivity and

a real interest in them as people. It means that if they never come
to know Jesus through our friendship, they are still friends.

Friendship evangelism seeks to meet people where they are.
The emphasis rightly deduces that it is unrealistic to expect
certain people to come to church, but rather rediscovers and
returns to the New Testament habit of proclaiming the good
news wherever they are. Why should I talk about friendship
evangelism in a book about hospitality? One reason is that
although friendships may start at the golf club, in the
company's dining room or down the pub, there's something
special about inviting a friend into your home.

In the mid-sixteenth century, John Calvin mourned the
demise of ancient hospitality: 'this office of humanity has . . .
nearly ceased to be properly observed amongst men . . . inns
now supply the place of accommodations for strangers.'[1] He
goes on to state that the dependence upon inns rather than personal hospitality is an expression of human depravity. A rather
extreme point of view, we would probably say, but the statement needs to be understood in the context of inns being one
of the ground-breaking innovations of sixteenth-century
society. Calvin, like many after him, saw such establishments as
a move down the slippery slope of impersonalisation and an
escape from a personal responsibility towards the stranger, the
poor or the traveller. It was thought that with this loss the
opportunity to influence and give witness to God's grace
through serving others had also been lost.

Somehow we open more of the 'package' of what it means
to be a Christian when we are seen in our own surroundings.
Much can be deduced about our value systems from the way we
behave in the home with our spouse and children. There's a
dynamic in the home that is different from the club or the pub.
It is that dynamic that is so beneficial for the non-Christian to
see, for that is Christianity in the raw. The home, with all its
inter-relationships, its social, economic and spiritual framework, is where true Christianity works. In the club and the pub
it will be mainly words and a few kind actions. A cynical non-

Christian could think it was counterfeit. But in the home, it will be nearer the real thing. Down through the ages Christians have often been accused of watering down the gospel to make it attractive. In the same way, and rather subtly, we can tend to be chameleon-like on neutral ground, to the point where others don't get a true picture of who we really are. We can all behave civilly in public, and indeed our behaviour may well change depending on who we are with. For instance, if we're playing golf with a potential business client, we may be more inclined to go the extra mile in our conduct than we would if we were playing an existing colleague. It's what I call the prelude to a catch syndrome. It's observed in every courtship, where there's tip-top manners until the catch has been secured. Once the deal is done, the marriage is promised, there is a relaxing of decorum. But at home, your spouse is unlikely to let you get away with any façade, so reality is more evident.

There's a dynamic in the home that is different from the club or the pub.

Another point to remember is that it can be difficult to share in a personal way about Jesus with a member of the opposite sex without our motives being misunderstood. If you are unmarried there is a risk of complicating motives. If you are married there's a risk of conflicting motives. We cannot always avoid the initial contacts, but bringing a friend of the opposite sex into the sphere of a mixed gathering or a family home is beneficial.

Prioritising time

If you are not in the habit of developing friendships in your recreation times or at your place of work, it will not be possible to start doing so without first making it a priority and reorganising your lifestyle. We may have the passion and desire to reach our neighbourhood for Jesus, but at the end of the day we have to realise that establishing friendships takes time; and time never presents itself, it has to be made. The reality is that many who have a heart for sharing the good news also have a servant heart in all aspects of church life. So prioritising your life so that time spent at home with the family and at work and at church is properly balanced, and yet still leaving time to establish new relationships, will inevitably mean that some things will have to be re-jigged or jettisoned completely.

Busy lives and work schedules can sometimes affect the way we think and make decisions. Rushed decisions in business can lead to costly results; rushed decisions about relationships can have disastrous effects. We take care to prioritise our time in relationships that will affect our business or personal lives, but what about relationships that may not affect us personally to the same extent but where the quality of time given may well influence someone else's decisions regarding eternity? The point is that we will always prioritise those things that are important to us, but we need to have the welfare and salvation of our neighbours higher up our agenda.

The life of faith needs to move up a gear if it's stuck as an optional extra.

Although individual Christians should lead the way in this, churches play an important role in ensuring members' time is not clogged up with church-based minutiae. My experience is that if members are busy in their community, the church morale is high. If they're too busy in church and don't have time in the community, not only is there decreased morale but any speaking tends to be negative back-biting rather than gospel sharing.

Good planning is probably the most important aspect of good time management. Plan ahead how you are going to reach your neighbours. Be imaginative in what you do: coffee mornings, joint projects, evening drinks or meals, jogging or walking the dog together, lifts to work or shopping. If we wait around to see what comes around, we won't be ready when or if it does! The life of faith needs to move up a gear if it's stuck as an optional extra on everything we do. Planning will ensure efficient and effective evangelism.

Find out what is going on in your neighbourhood. Does the local paper flag up anything that you could engage in and that could have an impact around you? What resources need to be considered? Analyse the issues and be prepared for them. Estimate the workload required, who does what and how long it will take. When we are thinking about ways to witness to our neighbours, estimating how much time will be needed is extremely important. If we underestimate, we will become depressed when a conversion hasn't happened within our time-frame. Always estimate for the long haul, for two reasons: you cannot really put a time on it, and second, we're not talking about pushing someone through a mechanical process; we're talking about relationship, and we want to befriend our neighbours whether or not they come to know Jesus within our lifetime.

Paradoxically, most busy people will tell us that it is astonishing how much we can fit into a day. This is often true, because when we have very little time we try to get as much as possible done in it, whereas when we have a lot of time we tend to relax more and therefore achieve less. The message from the way Jesus lived his life is that we are to make each minute count.

Friendships outside church

A few years ago I asked for a show of hands in my church congregation (about 250 people were present) as to how many had at least three non-Christian friends. Only 18 people put their hands up. 'What about two non-Christian friends?' I asked, and 45 people responded. 'One?' I said warily, and 86 people responded. That was not the high percentage I had expected from a charismatic evangelical fellowship. Here was an issue that needed to be addressed if we were going to make an impact in the local community. A closer look at the 18 revealed that they were also already heavily involved in other church activities.

How were we going to re-educate this church to see evangelism as a priority? Under scrutiny, the shape of our church schedule did not lend itself to evangelism. If we didn't address what we did on Sunday so that our services were more inviting and considerate towards the non-Christian, how could we expect people to adapt their own lives? Reformed behaviour needs examples. If it's true that the church is the only organisation that exists for its non-members, then we have to begin there.

If it's true that the church is the only organisation that exists for its non-members, then we have to begin there.

Our Sunday services assumed everyone was a believer. There would have been an intellectual and spiritual opposition to such a statement, but the fact was that the style, content and conduct of the 'members' all showed that we were acting as if all present knew exactly what was going on. We assumed all knew the language, the songs, the Bible passage, what prayer was, who was who, and a lot more besides. Three-quarters of an hour of worship to start the service was not very friendly for those who were not used to church, as they couldn't relate to it. If we wanted members to bring their friends, it was primarily because we wanted them to hear the gospel.

We altered the framework so that there was a quarter of an hour for worship, then the children went out and we had the message. We looked at our preaching styles and used a more interactive approach. Sometimes we had a choice of message style: one that catered for newcomers and another for more mature Christians. Both were interactive. Then we would come back together, often including the children, for a worship time that included a response to the message. If the children were studying similar things, and they often were, we would see if it were possible for them to participate in this part (remember, participating children bring non-participating parents). However, if non-Christians didn't want to sit through the worship time they were free to go, but they had heard the Scripture being taught and had often heard, rather surprisingly for some, Christians asking questions about their faith. So they discovered that Christians didn't know it all and often had the same dilemmas about living life!

Gene Edwards reminds us that 'love does not come about by [knowing that] "you have got to love one another". That love, and that camaraderie, that community, simply cannot come about by what is presently known as Sunday church.'[2] Another turning point for us was to cancel the evening service with the specific reason of creating time to invite neighbours to tea or supper, an afternoon walk together or whatever else was suitable. It was not a time to relish the fact that there was no evening service and we could watch TV instead. It was simply a different kind of 'service', with an evangelistic motive.

The other major change we made was to ensure that our house-group system catered for newcomers rather than just for established Christians. Pohl quotes the early eighteenth-century Methodists as 'having a significant but ambiguous role in the history of Christian hospitality. At a time when community ties were weakening, Methodist small group meetings offered regular opportunities for intense, personal interaction, relationship building and oversight of new believers.'[3] It was the rediscovery of these principles that led us to instigate groups that consisted of basic, welcoming homes for local groups to experience reality, fun, sometimes a meal or part of a meal, a short time of worship and study, which was adaptable depending on who came, and a time of sharing with a particular emphasis on the friends we were praying for. Obviously this time of sharing was handled very sensitively by the leader if non-Christians were present, but basically it did no harm to understand that here was a group of people who were concerned enough to pray for the needs of others outside the group. Then the evening would close with some prayer for the needs of those present.

> *The other major change we made was to ensure that our house-group system catered for newcomers.*

All these changes made way for people to live out their lives
with a view to how they could reach and befriend the people
who lived or worked alongside them.

I believe one of the most thought-changing passages of
Scripture in this regard is Acts 17:26: 'From one man he made
every nation of men, that they should inhabit the whole earth;
and he determined the times set for them and the exact places
where they should live.' The New King James version has, 'and
has determined their preappointed times and the boundaries of
their dwellings'. Most of us have sought the Lord about where
we are to live when a house move has been necessary, but do we
believe that not only will the Lord guide us to the right house
(an action that is predominantly concerned with self-interest)
but he has planned, in all of that, the people who will be our
neighbours and therefore those who will be the subject of our
'priestly duty' of evangelism?

This way of thinking puts witness and evangelism right into
the centre of our neighbourhood in a new way. If the position
of our house has been the subject of divine choice, then surely
the way we use our house is also part of God's plan. There is
nothing more thrilling, in our experience, than letting our
neighbours know that our back door is always open for them
and to find that they take us up on it. In the community we now
live in, it is one of our greatest joys that our neighbours will
often pop in for a drink and a chat simply because they were
passing.

Open house

As I have shared my thoughts with various people on the
subject matter of this book, it hasn't taken long for the issue of
'risk' and 'danger' to rear its head. Our homes are generally
more private and smaller than they used to be. 'Privacy
increases the risk involved in offering hospitality to strangers.
Both hosts and guests are more vulnerable when hidden from
view.'[4] Of course there are times when it's inconvenient, and

there are times when some will outstay if not their welcome then the reasonable timespan of their visit. When certain people make a habit of not knowing when or how to leave, you just need to be imaginative in laying down boundaries and being more assertive. If it's a Christian who has lingered too long, try asking, 'Shall we pray before you leave?' It seems to work well for us!

We might be tempted to look back at the good old days when everything was safer and such considerations were never given space in our thinking. It's interesting, then, that Martin Luther was convinced that Abraham and his sons had it easier in their day, because 'there was not such a large number of vagabonds and scoundrels in the world as there is today'.[5] One way to limit the risk with total strangers (most people from our neighbourhood or church do not fit into this category) is to begin our hosting at a church function or house-group setting. The ancient monastic communities were careful to emphasise the value of inviting strangers into 'a number of the daily rituals of monastic life'.[6]

PUTTING PRINCIPLES INTO PRACTICE

1. 'This office [hospitality] of humanity . . . has nearly ceased to be properly observed amongst men . . . inns now supply the place of accommodations for strangers.' Would you agree? To what extent can hospitality for strangers be redeemed?
2. Why did the early church meet in homes? Discuss the similarities and differences that exist today for the reasons you have given.
3. How important is it to have a hospitable home for a house group? And what would we really mean by that?
4. Have you had any experience of awkward guests when you have offered hospitality? Has it made you stop being hospitable? If not, what parameters have you set in place since?

5. Even though he was staying in someone else's house, Jesus used hospitality as a means of evangelism (John 1:39). List some imaginative ways in which you can use your home so that friends and neighbours can come and see Jesus.

6

Refreshing the Saints

May the Lord show mercy to the household of Onesiphorus,
because he often refreshed me and was not ashamed of my
chains. (2 Timothy 1:16)

The word 'refresh' means 'to reinvigorate; to restore something
that is lost'. This may be energy, general well-being or hope.
When a person is hot, cold, worn out or depressed, they need
refreshing, and that refreshment needs to be given to them from
outside themselves.

Refreshment at home

When we have been out and about and return home, or if we
visit a friend, there are socially acceptable practices that we
often engage in. In England the welcome will include, 'Let me
make you a cup of tea.' In other Western countries it might be,
'Let me fetch you a beer.' In ancient Israel it would have been,
'Let me bathe your feet.' All these are examples of the physical
refreshment we offer each other when we see the need.

Sometimes that refreshment is not in the home, but is as a
result of seeing a need and being thoughtful and proactive in
wanting to meet that need:

When David had gone a short distance beyond the summit, there
was Ziba, the steward of Mephibosheth, waiting to meet him. He
had a string of donkeys saddled and loaded with two hundred

loaves of bread, a hundred cakes of raisins, a hundred cakes of figs and a skin of wine. The king asked Ziba, 'Why have you brought these?' Ziba answered, 'The donkeys are for the king's household to ride on, the bread and fruit are for the men to eat, and the wine is to refresh those who become exhausted in the desert.' (2 Samuel 16:1–2)

Mephibosheth had plenty to be thankful to David for, and this 'mobile' hospitality was a way of demonstrating thanks. You will remember that one of the reasons for the command to be hospitable was that the Hebrews themselves had been strangers in the land. God had provided for their needs in many different ways, both miraculously and through others, so it's not surprising to find that refreshing each other is first seen in God's relationship with us.

Divine refreshment

Jeremiah 31 speaks of the new covenant that God will make with his people through the coming Messiah:

> This is what the LORD Almighty, the God of Israel, says: 'When I bring them back from captivity, the people in the land of Judah and in its towns will once again use these words: "The LORD bless you, O righteous dwelling, O sacred mountain." People will live together in Judah and all its towns – farmers and those who move about with their flocks. I will refresh the weary and satisfy the faint.' (Jeremiah 31:23)

God refreshes us. He is the greatest source of refreshment – physically, mentally and spiritually. So it will often be the case that a person who is refreshing to be with is a person who lives close to God and has been refreshed by him.

We need to understand that spiritual refreshment is of greater value than any other form of refreshment. When Jesus sent the disciples away to buy bread, they were surprised to hear him say when they returned that he had food they didn't

know anything about (John 4:32). He
had been witnessing to a Samaritan
woman (which surprised them too!) and
therefore had also been in communication and in harmony with his Father, and
that 'touching base' with his Father had
fed him spiritually.

*A person who is
refreshing to be
with is a person
who lives close to
God and has been
refreshed by him.*

The greatest need we have is to be
refreshed by God spiritually. If we refresh
others, our refreshment will also have a spiritual dimension,
and therefore our hospitality will become much more than
meeting physical hunger or social loneliness – the practice of
hospitality can make our homes a spiritual oasis for others.

Most of our understanding of refreshment has to do with
water, whether that's a desert pool, a bath or a cup of tea. Water
is a very precious commodity, especially in countries like Israel.
It has always been that way. It is surprising that a land flowing
with milk and honey should lack one of the fundamental ele-
ments of life, but it's the way God has chosen for his people to
learn to rely on him for the basic necessities.

Because of its rarity, villages only sprung up (excuse the
pun!) around water sources, so wells became the meeting place
for the community. It often became the 'town square' and was
therefore central to their lives. So when the Hebrews arrived at
a new place, they would first dig a well to see if they could tap
an underground spring. Jacob's well in Samaria is a good
example of that. If there was no well for the town then they
would build cisterns (Jeremiah 14:3). The problem with cisterns
is that if they become empty and dry due to drought, they
crack.

There are obvious spiritual analogies here. Solomon said,
'Above all else, guard your heart, for it is the wellspring of life'
(Proverbs 4:23). If we are not ourselves being refreshed by the
word of God, drought has come to us and we cannot give out
refreshing water. Jeremiah brings this heart-felt prophecy to
God's people: 'My people have committed two sins: They have

forsaken me, the spring of living water, and have dug their own cisterns, broken cisterns that cannot hold water' (Jeremiah 2:13).

The incident of Jesus at the well with the Samaritan woman in John 4 is an example of the well being at the centre of village life. John makes the point that this woman came at midday. Perhaps she came when everyone else was resting from the heat of the day because her lifestyle would have meant it was socially hard for her to interact with her neighbours. According to orthodox Judaism there were strict rules governing how a man and a woman could interact in public. A man was only able to ask a woman unknown to him for a drink. He could not instigate any further conversation, though it was acceptable for her to do so. The most likely place for such a scenario would be the village well, the most public place. So the circumstances of John 4 are very powerful from a social point of view: no one else was around except Jesus and the woman, she was a Samaritan, and Jews and Samaritans were not on speaking terms in Jesus' day, and yet they were conversing. Jesus began the conversation with the allowable phrase, 'Give me a drink.' The woman then continued conversing and the door was open for Jesus to share.

So the dynamics of refreshing and being refreshed, are at the heart of the ministry of hospitality.

The important thing to notice in this passage is that Jesus, staying within cultural expectations on an individual level as a courtesy, looked for and took every advantage to refresh this lady spiritually while she was invited to serve him. So the dynamics of giving and receiving, serving and sharing, refreshing and being refreshed, are at the heart of the ministry of hospitality.

Now, the path to refreshment isn't a doddle. Digging a well was hard work and after the digging was done, the daily walk to the well undertaken by the women of the household was not easy, especially on the way back when the 'jar' was full. These jars were long, cylindrical clay pots that were carried on the head. Some had two handles, cheaper ones had only one. There was a long rope with a leather bucket attached at each well, which was lowered down the well to reach the water, and they filled the large jars with the bucket. Because it was hard work, the day's supply of water was carried at twilight, in the cool of the evening, ready for the next day or first thing in the morning. As we've seen, the Samaritan woman went to the well at midday because she didn't want to meet anyone or hear any gossip about herself. It's good to know that even when your intention is to hide, Jesus can refresh you.

One of the most fascinating accounts of such hard work is that of Rachel feeding and watering the ten camels for Abraham's servant, who was on the look-out for a wife for his master's son Isaac. The servant used the same allowable phrase to speak to Rachel and asked for some more guidance (Genesis 24:14). If Abraham's servant was looking for a spiritually mature bride for Isaac, he'd found a spirituality with muscle! One camel can drink 182 litres!

The woman of Samaria was prepared to work to refresh Jesus, and her comment was that he didn't have anything to draw water with and the well was deep. (Because this was normally the job of the women, it also explains why it was easy for the disciples to find the upper room where the Passover was to be kept, because Jesus had instructed them to look for a *man* carrying a jar of water: this would have been a relatively rare sight.) The Jews had two 'nicknames' for water. First, 'the gift of God', because of its rarity and its enormous value for life. Second, they called it 'living water' because running water means that it is fresh and not stagnant. Jesus developed both those themes in his conversation with the woman at the well, when he replied, 'Whoever drinks the water I give him will never thirst again.'

Spiritual refreshment for one another

Hospitality is both God's gift and a living opportunity to refresh and be refreshed. We should not back off from the ministry of refreshing others when it looks as if it will involve hard work, because it's a ministry where both host and guest will be refreshed.

In Ephesus, Paul had been debating with the Jews about Jesus being the Messiah. He had done this for three months in the synagogue, and Onesiphorus, realising the toll this had taken on Paul, had found ways to refresh him. In like manner we are to encourage and refresh others through the power of gentle words, gracious gifts and generally being the fragrance of Christ. Solomon wrote: 'He who refreshes others will himself be refreshed' (Proverbs 11:25). Just as benefactors used to walk through the streets giving away food and drink to the poor, God searches for those who would quench the spiritual thirst of those needing encouragement and affirmation.

Onesiphorus was interested in the lives of others. We can see in 2 Timothy 1:17 that when he went to Rome, he searched hard for Paul. His life was not consumed with merely his own concerns; he was also committed to encouraging others. We may not be able to pronounce his name, but we do need to imitate this characteristic of Onesiphorus and seek ways to serve and refresh one another by caring, adopting a non-judgemental attitude and having a ready shoulder to cry on as needed.

Henry Ford, the first great production-line car manufacturer, was once asked, 'Who is your best friend?' On a tablecloth he scribbled, 'He is your best friend who brings out of you the best that is in you.' That is what it means to refresh others: to be vessels that bring out the best possible character in others and encourage them to walk as sons and daughters of God. It is expected that Christians will persevere in this kind of activity.

One of the most challenging statements of Jesus is that in the last days 'the love of most will grow cold' (Matthew 24:12). The word for 'love' in this passage is *agape*, rarely used outside the New Testament, as the Greeks thought it unattainable. The word is used in Scripture to describe God's love for mankind and a Christian's love for his fellow men. It is unconditional, undeserved love. But here we are told that this love that we should exhibit towards each other will wane in the last days. Then Jesus adds, 'But he who stands firm to the end will be saved.'

One way to refresh one another is to show that we care. In Scripture, the idea of care has largely to do with an interest in other people. It is descriptive of Paul's phrase, 'Each of you should look not only to your own interests, but also to the interests of others' (Philippians 2:4). The predominant New Testament usage involves the mind; it's thinking about other people.

'I can live for two months on one good compliment.'

It seems to me that to think 'encouragement' is the key, for if we are truly encouragers we will naturally love and care for one another. Mark Twain once said, 'I can live for two months on one good compliment.' Encouragement fortifies people, for amazing things can be done on the strength of encouragement. In the battle against the Benjamites, the Israelites, having just lost 22,000 on the battlefield in one day, 'encouraged one another and again took up their positions' (Judges 20:22). They knew how to keep up the morale in times of difficulty.

It is no wonder then that the persecuted church, longing for the Second Coming of the Lord, is told to encourage one another with the facts of the Scriptures (1 Thessalonians 4:13–18; 5:9–11). We are called especially to encourage the oppressed (Isaiah 1:17), the timid (1 Thessalonians 5:14) and young men to be self-controlled (Titus 2:6). The oppressed, because they need understanding, support and commitment so that they are not alone as they fight the spiritual battles that will bring them deliverance. The timid, because others always play a large part in building or re-establishing confidence. And the young men, because to train and disciple young people is a valuable task for the future, and to lose them and their zeal because they are not self-controlled would be a sad loss indeed.

The writer to the Hebrews on several occasions calls his readers to encourage one another: 'See to it . . . that none of you has a sinful, unbelieving heart that turns away from the living God. But encourage one another daily . . . so that none of you may be hardened by sin's deceitfulness' (Hebrews 3:12–13); 'Let us not give up meeting together, as some are in the habit of doing, but let us encourage one another – and all the more as you see the Day approaching' (10:25).

Barnabas was nicknamed 'Son of Encouragement' by the apostles. In Acts 4:37 there is an example of his encouragement. The church was being led by the Holy Spirit to lay their possessions at the feet of the apostles so that there was no one in need within the fellowship. The church numbered well over 3,000, but Barnabas's contribution was the only one mentioned, probably because he led the way as an encouragement to others to follow suit. If we are encouragers, we won't want to hang about waiting for others to do the right thing first; we'll get in there and do it, whatever others may think.

Barnabas saw the best in people too. Nobody among the disciples in Jerusalem was prepared to believe that Saul, the most feared persecutor of the church, had become a Christian. Saul had tried in vain to contact the believers, but had been held in suspicion. But Barnabas testified that in Damascus Paul had preached the gospel fearlessly. It is a great gift and ministry to be able to see the hand of the Lord on a person and affirm them.

The ministry of encouragement does not consist merely of nice words to bolster up a person. Sometimes it can mean standing with them in the face of rejection, danger and opposition, even to the point of losing one's own credibility.

All around us there are people who have had no church background coming to know Jesus personally. Some have been involved in the occult, some in immoral practices, but whatever the past has held for them, their future will be determined largely by those who represent Christ here on earth, the church. Will we see the best in them, refresh them and affirm them in the ministry that God would give them?

Encouragement is a gift of the Holy Spirit, a 'charismata', that is singled out in Romans 12:8. It is not one of the demonstrative gifts, but that doesn't mean it is any less important. If the Lord has given you the gift of encouragement then, Paul says, encourage. In other words, encourage for all you're worth! It may be a special gift for some, but we are all called to encourage, for we all know the reality of life's hardships. Barnabas encourages all followers of Jesus by reminding them that in order to enter the kingdom of God they must 'go through many hardships' (Acts 14:22).

PUTTING PRINCIPLES INTO PRACTICE

1. Describe an occasion when you have been refreshed, physically and spiritually.
2. In what ways can we refresh each other on a regular basis? How many of the things on your list will involve others coming to your home?
3. Are there other characteristics that go hand in hand with someone who refreshes others? If you think there are, what are they?
4. Describe the characteristics of an imaginary person who does not refresh others.

7

Who Is My Neighbour?

In the field of world policy I would dedicate this nation to
the policy of the good neighbour.

(Franklyn D. Roosevelt, first inaugural address,
4th March 1933)

We have seen that biblical law specified that it was an obligation
to extend hospitality and love to the 'alien' or 'stranger', for the
Hebrew people themselves were once 'aliens [*gerim*] in Egypt'
(Leviticus 19:34). Isaiah says that a genuinely righteous person
will fulfil the obligation to 'share your food with the hungry and
to provide the poor wanderer with shelter' (Isaiah 58:7). Job, in
his own defence, claims, 'No stranger had to spend the night in
the street, for my door was always open to the traveller' (Job
31:32). The term used in rabbinic literature for hospitality is
haknasat orhim; literally, 'bringing in of guests' or 'gathering in
of travellers'.

'Neighbour', according to the Oxford English Dictionary
definition, is 'a dweller next door, near, in same street or village
or district, or in adjacent country especially regarded as one
who should be friendly or as having a claim on others' friendli-
ness'. That is a pretty wide definition, yet we are encouraged to
see even more in it within Scripture. The Bible tells us that God,
through his servant Moses, commanded the Jews to love their
neighbour (Leviticus 19:18). James later called this the 'royal
law' (James 2:8). When Jesus was asked by the lawyer what he
had to do to attain eternal life, Jesus asked the lawyer how he
interpreted the laws of God handed down through Moses, to

which he replied, '"Love the Lord your God with all your heart and with all your soul and with all your strength and with all your mind" and, "Love your neighbour as yourself."' Impressed by his answer, Jesus said to him, 'You have answered correctly . . . Do this and you will live.' Then the lawyer asked, 'And who is my neighbour?' (see Luke 10:25–29).

In reply, Jesus told the well-known parable of the Good Samaritan. The story says that a man, travelling from Jerusalem to Jericho, was mugged and left for dead. A priest and a Levite, representing those who should be among the most caring, both passed by on the other

The question 'Who is my neighbour?' caused endless disputes.

side. However, when a Samaritan (from a race traditionally despised and considered outcasts) approached and saw the condition of the wounded stranger, he took him to a resting place and nursed him. He had to continue his journey the next day, but he left some money with the owner of the inn to cover any expenses in looking after the injured stranger, promising to pay off the balance on his return. After telling his story, Jesus asked the lawyer, 'Which of these three do you think was a neighbour to the man who fell into the hands of robbers?' The lawyer answered, 'The one who had mercy on him.' Jesus said to him, 'Go and do likewise' (Luke 10:25–37).

Among the Jews the question 'Who is my neighbour?' caused endless disputes. There was no doubt as to who the Samaritans were; it wasn't that they were simply the inhabitants of the place known as Samaria – they had a history. These people remained in the cities of Samaria after the captivity of Israel by Shalmaneser in 721 BC, creating a tension and hatred between these two people groups. When the Jews eventually returned from captivity they didn't allow the Samaritans to participate in the rebuilding of the temple at Jerusalem, and the continued friction that followed meant that from that time they became open enemies.

So for Jesus to include in his teaching a parable that showed a Samaritan in a good light was a proverbial 'red rag', to say the least. History dictated the Jewish attitude towards these people. John, the gospel writer, highlights the main difference between the Jews and the Samaritans as a difference in religious belief. It was the issue of what constitutes true worship (John 4:19f). The Pharisees found nothing good to say about the Samaritans, and instead they poured out curses on them. The strength of the division between the two is seen in the Samaritan woman's response to Jesus' request for a drink: 'You are a Jew and I am a Samaritan woman. How can you ask me for a drink?' 'For,' adds John, 'Jews do not associate with Samaritans' (John 4:9).

The priest and the Levite would have been worshipping in the temple within hours of coming across the victim in this story. Why did they then neglect the special opportunity that God presented to them to bless a fellow human being, thereby demonstrating their love for him? None of us can be sure of their reasons. Jesus uses the picture of one of the most hated helping one of the Jews' most vulnerable people, but he could have cited other issues on the neighbourhood front for these religiously exclusive Jewish legal experts. They also had questions about where the distinction should be made among the people of their own nation and among the different classes of society. Who should the priest, the rabbi and the elder regard as a neighbour? The Jews spent their lives in various religious ceremonies and any contact with those who did not share that religion, the ignorant and the careless, would cause defilement. Surely they weren't to regard the 'unclean' as neighbours?

Are we immune from making similar wrong deductions? Not at all. For example, it's possible for us, as Christians, to separate the holy from the mundane for different reasons. The Greek-influenced West tends to create a wide chasm between the secular and the sacred – a chasm that just doesn't exist in Hebrew biblical thinking. The West believes that if you have a physical problem it shouldn't affect your spiritual life, and if you have a spiritual problem it shouldn't affect you physically. But the Scripture doesn't see it like that. The psalmist says:

Blessed is the man whose sin the LORD does not count against him and in whose spirit is no deceit. When I kept silent, my bones wasted away through my groaning all day long. For day and night your hand was heavy upon me; my strength was sapped as in the heat of summer. Then I acknowledged my sin to you and did not cover up my iniquity. I said, 'I will confess my transgressions to the LORD – and you forgave the guilt of my sin.' (Psalm 32:2–5)

On another occasion the psalmist says, 'Because of your wrath there is no health in my body; my bones have no soundness because of my sin' (Psalm 38:3). These verses demonstrate that the spiritual and the physical are so interlocked that they affect each other. Our failure to recognise how the two are related has meant that, consciously or subconsciously, there is a tendency to split our spiritual lives from our physical lives. One part of our lives is made up of great things, the focus being on the worship of God; the other part is made up of so-called little things, in which the command 'You shall love your neighbour as yourself' might be part. It is perfectly possible that after worship on a Sunday we might ignore the victim of an assault. We might even justify it on the basis that we have planned a restful, truly Sabbath-type time at home with the family.

We might neglect the needs of others from a different motive. Some believe they are working in the cause of Christ, seeking to build up some worthy enterprise on a large, wider scale. They feel that they are doing a great work, and they cannot stop to notice the wants of the needy and distressed. But to spend all our energy on some apparently great work, while we neglect the needy or turn the stranger away, is not a service that will meet with God's approval.

Jesus made it clear that being a neighbour means anyone who loves, helps and does good things to another without expecting anything in return, even to those he does not know, and to those who might be considered outcasts, inferior or enemies. We see this in action as all over the world, missions, charitable organisations and individuals bring relief and hope to others who have been affected by the earth's calamities and disasters.

Peter, emphasising the importance of good neighbourliness, said, 'Love one another deeply, from the heart' (1 Peter 1:22). The love of our neighbours should be free of hypocrisy, and requires adherence to Jesus' instruction that we should act as we would want others to act towards us.

Britain is now a multilingual, multi-ethnic, multicultural and multifaith nation, and these developments bring into play our current issues of asylum, racial justice and relationships between faiths. For some, recognition of these changes in Britain over the past few decades has had a dislocating and unsettling effect. For others there is frustration that achieving a realistic racial justice and an acceptance of diversity is taking far too long. Complicated issues like these either bring new light or they arouse fear. They can enrich our lives or they can be divisive.

We cannot touch base with the divine without touching base with humanity.

Diversity is a fundamental of our culture today and in many ways that makes it rather special. As a nation we have moved forward in countering racism, and we are learning, slowly, to celebrate our differences. We are also dialoguing with other faiths creatively, though much more remains to be done.

Love is the basis of true spirituality and no one can show pure love towards God unless he has unselfish love for his brother. It is not possible for the heart in which Christ abides to be destitute of love. If we love God because he first loved us, we shall love all whom Christ died for. We cannot touch base with the divine without touching base with humanity.

Wherever there is an impulse of love and sympathy reaching out to bless others, there is the working of God's Holy Spirit: 'Whatever you did for one of the least of these brothers of mine, you did for me' (Matthew 25:40). We must learn to anticipate the sorrows, difficulties and troubles of others; to enter into the joys and sorrows of the rich and poor of all races. 'Freely you have received,' Jesus says, 'freely give' (Matthew

10:8). All around us there are those in need who would benefit from our sympathising words and helpful deeds.

Neighbours yet strangers

The experience of being an outsider or stranger is not restricted to people living far from their own country. In our growing cosmopolitan twenty-first-century society we are surrounded every day by people whose skin and accent remind us that we all experience the uncharted events that can make us strangers in our own country and even in our own families. For personal, political, religious or just professional reasons, someone can feel distanced from, or even rejected by, his family or people. The psalmist alludes to this when he's persecuted for his faithfulness to God: 'I am a stranger to my brothers, an alien to my own mother's sons' (Psalm 69:8).

Jesus probably felt like an outsider when he declared that 'no prophet is accepted in his home town' (Luke 4:24). Condemned to death and rejected by the Jewish authorities, unjustly persecuted like the psalmist, he was perhaps the outsider *par excellence*.

Moreover, we can also feel alienated from ourselves. Which of us has never felt at odds with himself? We often act or speak in a way we later regret. The apostle Paul describes this weird feeling of disunity within himself: 'I do not understand what I do. For what I want to do I do not do, but what I hate I do . . . For what I do is not the good I want to do; no, the evil I do not want to do – this I keep on doing' (Romans 7:15, 19). It is in understanding how close loneliness is to our own constitution that enables us to identify at least the external causes of loneliness in others.

The loneliness that we experience after moving house, starting a new job, beginning a new course in school or college, being stopped by the police (guilty or not), visiting a new church, shopping at an unfamiliar store – all these and many more – is something that often throws us onto the hospitality of those who are familiar with that situation and those for whom there is now no strangeness.

From the other side, to look out for strangers in these situations may not normally be on our minds once we ourselves are settled. But the call to hospitality includes the reminder to be aware of those who are unsettled in our immediate neighbourhood, in church, at work – in fact, anywhere we feel safe and all is familiar. This is 'because you yourselves were once strangers'.

Who are these strangers? They may be those suffering from lack of a place that is 'home', they may be strangers to us because of their habits, such as drugs or alcohol, or their sexual bias. Is there a way for the Christian community to demonstrate that we are those who welcome strangers, whatever their history, whatever their needs?

Like all people, these strangers may well be alienated from themselves. For those who come from abroad it's even harder to escape their own inner contradictions because they are distanced from the background of family, culture and religion. This factor can complicate our relationship with them and might even increase the risk of it turning into a relationship based on power. That's why foreigners can easily become scapegoats, where they become the object of blame for everything wrong in our society. So rather than welcoming them we might find ourselves wanting to dominate or even ill-treat them.

The people of Sodom were known for treating visitors harshly and indifferently, and perhaps one of their motives was to discourage others wanting to settle among them. John Wesley thought there was a huge social gap between those who practised and those who avoided hospitality, which supports the dubious motives of the people of Sodom:

One great reason why the rich in general have so little sympathy for the poor is because they seldom visit them. Hence it is (according to the common observation) one part of the world does not know what the other suffers. Many of them do not know, because they do not care to know: they keep out of the way of knowing it – and

then plead their voluntary ignorance as an exuse for their hardness
of heart.[1]

Surely we do not want to be like that? It is not always easy to
offer the hospitality that God requires, but I believe that God,
in whose image we were made, gave us creative minds and the
necessary power to think of humane responses to such human
needs.

This is why the law laid down by Moses contains detailed
teaching concerning 'aliens' and strangers. The teaching is
underlined by most of the Old Testament prophets, who
remind the Israelites how they should behave towards strangers. The same prophets warned about being taken captive and
exiled, and then spoke into the horrors of exile when it actually
happened.

The greater the difference between the home country and the
new country, the more moving into the new country seems like
going into exile. Sometimes this feeling of being in exile will
motivate people to endeavour to integrate into their new
society. But more often it has the opposite effect and makes
them vulnerable, in some cases even to the point of criminal
activity.

So to the question 'Who is the stranger?' the answer is any
whom Jesus himself would seek to minister to: 'For I was
hungry and you gave me something to eat, I was thirsty and you
gave me something to drink, I was a stranger and you invited
me in' (Matthew 25:35).

If, therefore, foreigners are vulnerable, and if God is full of
compassion for them, what should our responsibility as
Christians be towards them? I will look at this in greater detail
in Chapter 9 'Strangers on our Shores', but here are some considerations.

Respecting their rights

Foreigners, like us, are created in God's image and therefore are
worthy of respect. The Jews were instructed: 'Do not oppress

an alien; you yourselves know how it feels to be aliens, because
you were aliens in Egypt' (Exodus 23:9). Demonstrating a
respect for foreigners means in the first place respecting their
basic rights. The Bible especially mentions the right to a fair
wage (Deuteronomy 24:14–15) and access to unbiased justice
(Leviticus 24:22; Deuteronomy 1:16; 24:17; 27:19).

Treating them like one of us

'When an alien lives with you in your land, do not ill-treat
him. The alien living with you must be treated as one of your
native-born. Love him as yourself, for you were aliens in
Egypt' (Leviticus 19:33–34; Deuteronomy 10:19). From this we
can draw two conclusions: first, the foreigner is also a neighbour, even though he may not share our background, culture
and religion. Second, if the Israelites had to take special care of
the foreigners because of their particular circumstances, we
should show similar care and concern for those living around
us.

Loving foreigners as ourselves will mean coming to their aid
when they are in need, demonstrating a loving attitude towards
them and overcoming the prejudices held against them. The
onus is on us, the host, to take the initiative in making contact,
as Jesus did with the Samaritan woman, so as to break down
any perceived barriers between us. This kind of response to our
foreign neighbours may well mean accepting that we are going
to be rejected by those who do not favour our welcome of them.

Sharing the gospel

Our Christian duty to befriend foreigners includes the responsibility to show them the love of God in Christ Jesus. Perhaps
we could say, from a divine perspective, that the very reason
they have come to our neighbourhood is so that we may be the
catalyst of the gospel to them.

God intended his salvation for all the peoples of the earth.
This is illustrated in the Old Testament in the covenant made
with Abraham (Genesis 17:5f), and the covenant with the

people of Israel, which included all the foreigners living in Israel (Deuteronomy 29:10ff; 31:12). In fact, all the major prophets of Israel speak of the day when people will come from the ends of the earth to worship the God of the universe (Isaiah 56:6f). The gospel is good news for all people.

In the New Testament, the Jewish Messiah had a conversation with a foreigner when he spoke with the Samaritan woman (John 4). It was a very personal conversation, where Jesus showed how to both listen and respond to someone often despised and estranged from others. We must learn how to get to know foreigners, to understand them, so that what we say will resonate for them, addressing their concerns and questions.

Humility towards foreigners is necessary if we want to enter into a relationship with them. The most common Old Testament word for humility means 'to be lowly, submissive and modest'. The opposite would be to impose our religion, our culture or our ideas upon them.

Of course, it will not always be easy to communicate the gospel to people whose culture is different from our own, but there are the rewards of seeing some thinking more intelligently about the gospel, some making commitments to follow Jesus as Lord and Saviour and, just as important, our own beliefs become sharpened and more ordered so that we too grow in our knowledge of the Lord.

Creative local neighbourhood action

Following the Queen's Silver Jubilee and then the Golden Jubilee celebrations it was frequently observed that people discovered, often for the first time, who their neighbours were. People spoke of partying, of neighbourliness, of new friendships, of a sense of camaraderie and of belonging. If they spoke like that in 1977, and to a slightly lesser extent in 2002, it does beg the question why nobody thought to find ways of re-creating that atmosphere in the intervening 25 years! The fact is that what made them experience those good qualities and benefits of having neighbours was a focus. If that is so, what focus might be found in everyday living among the same neighbours?

I have found in the neighbourhoods where I have lived that there is one focus common to most: the desire to 'do up' the home. The time and energy people put into smartening up their homes inside and out these days is unprecedented. The DIY age has surely come to maturity. On a bank holiday you can be sure that two kinds of store will always be open: DIY stores and the garden centres. I am a DIY boffin myself, so this is a point of particular interest to me. The question we could or should ask is 'Could we not share some of the tools needed for these jobs?' If I see my neighbour in and out of his garden shed, I will go and find out what project is being undertaken and, if appropriate, offer any tools I might have that would help him do the job more accurately or quickly. If this is a neighbour I haven't spoken to very often, this could actually be a ground-breaking conversation, and it's about something we have in common.

I have been politely rebuffed in this once or twice, but nevertheless the door has been opened into a new relationship. More often than not the offer is well received, and experience, tools and sometimes labour are shared. In our last home our immediate neighbour, whom we knew pretty well, once knocked on our door and said to my wife, 'Is Paddy in?' and followed this with: 'It's Paddy the carpenter I'm after, not Paddy the pastor.' Paddy the pastor had had opportunities to minister to this neighbour and his wife when their daughter was diagnosed with cancer, and on other occasions. We had taken them to some evangelistic events at the church too, but at this moment he needed other help, practical help. On this occasion we replaced his garage door together using some of my tools. In both pastoral and practical spheres I had been able to be a neighbour, and that was a privilege.

In that particular neighbourhood, four of our neighbours had often joined forces on some jobs: drainage, pruning, preparing for a new drive. The level of friendship that we enjoyed fashioned some new thinking in me: could we not share the cost of contractors to do common tasks?

Every year I noticed that a few neighbours had hired contractors to prune their biggest trees, or renew the tarmac or paving on their drive, but had used either different contractors or the same contractor at different times. I approached the neighbours and suggested that in the spring we all gather together and pool our plans for the summer DIY jobs, so that we could use the same contractor for similar jobs and thereby get a reduction on the costs. But it wasn't just the financial benefits that I was looking at; it was the fact that in order to plan properly it would mean one or two meetings together – meetings where we could have a drink and some cake and in this hospitable environment make our decisions together. I live in a more rural area now, but one thing I have recently discovered is that several in the village buy from the same supplier, so we telephone each other when we place an order from a company where we probably only want a handful of things but postage is free if the order exceeds a certain amount.

The DIY age has surely come to maturity.

Neighbourhood Watch has had similar benefits of drawing neighbours together over a common concern. It's simply a matter of spending a little time thinking along these lines. Another government-led initiative has been to encourage car-sharing. I have had no experience of this because travelling to the church office rarely follows a set pattern. The incentive from the government's point of view is an economic and practical one. The reasoning is that if I give my neighbour a lift to work, we save petrol. If I have saved 45 litres of petrol, I have prevented 22 cubic metres of carbon dioxide from being released into the atmosphere.

There is of course a very good social reason for car-sharing too: we get to know one another better. Will it ever catch on? I believe we need to see changes in much more foundational

behaviour first. We have to learn to be less fanatical about our
own space. Happily, I have never had to commute by train on
a regular basis, but I have done the occasional trip at peak
commuter times. Did I say fanatical about our own space? Rail
commuters in Britain are a special breed. I know of nowhere
else in Europe where a crowded carriage can be so quiet, with
every head bowed in a newspaper or book and every eye religiously avoiding the gaze of others!

PUTTING PRINCIPLES INTO PRACTICE

1. Who might be present-day 'Samaritans' in our society?
2. How much has our thinking indoctrinated us about other
    races because of different historical events or teaching?
3. How would you know if your neighbour was lonely?
4. Discuss the balance needed between helping a lonely person
    and enabling them to keep a healthy independence.
5. What do your neighbours spend time doing? Discuss some
    joint projects you could see working among your neigh-
    bours.

8

Praying for our Neighbours

We do not know what we ought to pray for, but the Spirit
himself intercedes for us. (Romans 8:26)

An important part of our ministry of hospitality is to remember our neighbours and friends in prayer. In doing so, we may
find the Holy Spirit opens new doors for us, or gives us a spirit
of wisdom and knowledge for their individual circumstances so
that our hospitality can truly touch their lives.

Paul himself admitted that we just do not know what to pray
for (Romans 8:26), and this is often the case when wanting to
know exactly how to pray for one another. Having stated that,
there are a number of things we do know from Scripture that
can very easily form a framework or a tool for our praying for
one another. For instance, one of the best frameworks for
prayer is the one Jesus himself taught us. Some have taken the
view that this is simply a prayer to be prayed, but others feel it
is a framework to concentrate the mind – a series of headings
for us to expand on in prayer to our heavenly Father as part of
our relationship with him. Moreover, such a prayer is not just
to be prayed for ourselves. It also forms a suitable structure for
praying for our brothers and sisters in the body, so that rather
than 'give us this day our daily bread', we pray, 'Give them this
day their daily bread; deliver them from evil, enable them to
forgive as you have forgiven them . . .'

One of the things that we tend to do when we pray for other

people is to say, 'Lord, bless them . . .' That is a very general prayer, but it is only as we pray specifically that the Lord can answer our prayers directly. Watching for specific prayers to be answered is a valuable part of relationship with each other, and therefore it is to be recommended when praying for our neighbours. Clearly, our prayers can become more specific as we get to know our neighbours better, but inevitably our prayers for them will start as more general ones.

Paul's prayers for those to whom he was writing his letters can serve as good outlines. In Ephesians 1 Paul lists the spiritual blessings that we have in Christ. So pray that your neighbours too may be blessed with a peace that passes all understanding, joy that stems from salvation, hope for the future, wisdom to understand the things of God and patience.

Paul often prays for the wisdom of God for those to whom he writes. He prays that they may 'abound more and more in knowledge and depth of insight', that they 'may be able to discern what is best' (Philippians 1:9–10); that they may know God's will; that they may have all spiritual wisdom and understanding; that they may grow in the knowledge of God (Colossians 1:9).

It seems that Paul is conscious of the fact that there is a limit to how much he can teach his readers, and how much he can pass on to them and enthuse them. For the Christian life is not a matter of listening to others and imitating others (important as that is). It's more to do with working out our own salvation with fear and trembling (Philippians 2:12) and developing a relationship with God whereby we come to know him personally and intimately.

There are times when Paul points out to his readers their failings – their wrong-doing and wrong-saying – and that is only right and to be expected from an apostle. But he is well aware that the only thing that will change a person is their own walk with God. In our relationships with non-Christians around us we must take note of this fact, and however much we may wish to point the finger and tell other people where they are wrong and how they should change, we must refrain from doing so. The greatest need is to ask the Lord to step in. He can do things much more effectively, much more powerfully, much more gently, much more graciously than we could ever do. And more than that, our relationship with the one we are praying for isn't complicated by any negative thoughts of how we have viewed them! So if we really care about them, we will be praying that they may receive that spirit of wisdom and a revelation that their hearts may be enlightened so that they themselves receive from God himself knowledge of any areas in their lives that need addressing.

Paul goes on to pray that they may be filled with hope and the riches of his glorious inheritance. He is expressing his expectations that we should be people who are positive in our outlook because we have a living hope. It's a prayer linked to salvation, of course, but it's the heart of God that none of his creation should live with their heads hung in confusion about the life he has given them. This hope will not only be the motivation for their life but will be, when they've come to know Jesus personally, their motivation for the gospel and the discovery of the glorious inheritance that is theirs because of their belief.

In Ephesians 3:14ff Paul prays that his readers may be strengthened by Christ, and that they would know that Christ dwells in their hearts and they would be rooted and established in love. The prayerful desire that Jesus should dwell in their hearts is one that demonstrates Paul's belief that Jesus should influence everything we say or do. To pray that others may know Christ dwelling within them is to be praying that they may be conscious that he enables them to win through every problem; that he watches every move, every word, every thought, and he wills them to behave in a godly way. It is to pray that they may be motivated by holiness rather than selfishness.

To pray that his readers may be rooted and established in love is to pray that they may be aware of the divine intention that they be secure in God's love, and as a result demonstrate that same unconditional love to their neighbours. For if we are established in love, it will show in all our actions and reactions towards one another. This is a road of discovery that stretches in every direction, for there's a height, length, depth and breadth to God's love for us to experience which eventually will equate to a fullness of love. I can only think of this as being completely enveloped, filled to overflowing and saturated in God's love.

If we are praying for one another like this in the church, the home and our place of work – that we may be filled with God's love – it is unlikely that there will be the bickering, negative thoughts, destructive undercurrents and speaking against one another (especially leaders) that so easily ruins the living environment of those places and rather destroys the good things Jesus wants us to experience. And if we're praying for our unbelieving neighbours like this, it is unlikely that we will harbour any wrong preconceived ideas about them that might delay or totally prevent good relationships developing between us.

When we're faced with certain situations, it is not easy to know how we should be praying, especially when it involves someone we don't know that well. When there is a breakdown in a marriage, or when a person doesn't have a job, how do we discern what is best? We may know what we would like, but is it God's best? There is one way through this that I have found to be most helpful; it is to pray about how we should pray. Prayer about praying is often a foundation for more effective prayer. It throws us upon God rather than trot out a form of prayer that has worked in the past. I don't believe that God is a God of formula. He is a God of personal relationship, both with the pray-er and the one being prayed for. Since everyone is different and their life's path is unique, we can be certain that the way we should be praying will not be exactly the same way as we prayed for someone in a similar situation last week, though some aspects of the prayer might be similar.

So learn to pray about prayer. If we pray for the gift of wisdom and the gift of knowledge, we are more likely to pray in a way that is divinely inspired. Paul encourages every believer to discern for themselves what is best. He is not in the business of trying to work out everyone's problems for them. He wants us to learn to develop our relationship, our hearing of the divine whisper. We are too tempted to follow formulas and formats, too ready to opt for the safety of what has already been done. It's a way of thinking that permeates many aspects of church life.

Learn to pray about prayer.

We might argue that there's no point in reinventing the wheel, or 'if it's not broke don't fix it', but to pursue this line of thinking as spiritual people destroys two great divine fundamentals. It destroys the creativity that is planted in us all by the Creator who made us in his image, and, second, it destroys our calling to listen to God for ourselves.

Neighbourhood 'watch and pray'

The Jews, like the Greeks and Romans, divided the night hours into military watches, each watch representing the period for which sentinels or pickets remained on duty. The Jews recognised only three watches: the beginning of the watches, which was sunset to 2200 hours (Lamentations 2:19), the middle watch, 2200–0200 hours (Judges 7:19), and the morning watch or last watch, which covered 0200 hours to sunrise (Exodus 14:24). After the Romans enforced their supremacy, the number of watches was increased to four, and they were described according to their numerical order, for example the 'fourth watch' (Matthew 14:25), or by the terms 'even', 'midnight', 'cock-crowing' and 'morning' (see Mark 13:35). These terminated respectively at 2100 hours, midnight, 0300 hours and 0600 hours.

Matthew 26:40–41 records the time when Jesus returns to his disciples and finds them sleeping: '"Could you men not keep watch with me for one hour?" he asked Peter. "Watch and pray so that you will not fall into temptation. The spirit is willing, but the body is weak."'

We all know something about prayer. But what about watching? A clue to how Jesus understood the true meaning of 'watch' can be found in Jesus' comments in Matthew 26:41, 'The spirit is willing, but the body is weak.' It would seem that watching involves bodily strength. But it is a strength that we need to find if we are not to miss what Jesus might say to us.

Peter, James and John failed to watch on the mountain of

It is clear that there are times in our lives which are key.

Transfiguration when Jesus appeared with Moses and Elijah. At that time Jesus tried to speak to these three disciples about his future (Luke 9:28–36), but they fell asleep and missed what Jesus was telling them. In the Garden of Gethsemane, Peter, James and John again fell asleep at a time when prayer was crucial (Matthew 26:36–46). It is clear that there are times in our lives which are key; significant events when God would call us to be especially alert so as not to miss the battle.

When the apostle Peter wrote his two letters to the early church he often reflected on his own failures in his experience with Jesus and, learning from his own failure to 'watch', he encouraged his readers to learn to be watchful: 'The end of all things is near. Therefore be clear minded and self-controlled so that you can pray' (1 Peter 4:7).

But it's at this point that we can easily fall into guilt and close our ears to anything else, because not only have we failed to 'watch' as well as pray, but we know we shall often do so. We do, of course, need to learn to watch by keeping abreast of world affairs and alert to what is going on around us so that we don't become complacent and lose the cutting edge of effective praying. But at the same time, we mustn't fall into the trap that if we fail in our watching we have become useless pray-ers and God will pass us by. A few who are particularly called to intercession can have a knack of making others feel guilty about their lack of attendance at all-night prayer meetings. But I do not see that attitude in Jesus when the disciples fell asleep:

'Watch and pray so that you will not fall into temptation. The spirit
is willing, but the body is weak.' He went away a second time and
prayed, 'My Father, if it is not possible for this cup to be taken away
unless I drink it, may your will be done.' When he came back, he
again found them sleeping, because their eyes were heavy. So he left
them and went away once more and prayed the third time, saying
the same thing. Then he returned to the disciples and said to them,
'Are you still sleeping and resting? Look, the hour is near, and the
Son of Man is betrayed into the hands of sinners. Rise, let us go!
Here comes my betrayer!' (Matthew 26:41–46)

When Jesus notes that they are asleep, I don't get the feeling
that he's tutting under his breath as he returns to prayer. He
checks again later and a third time returns to prayer without
them, but there's no sense of resentment or anger against them.
You could say that his comment about the Spirit being willing
and the flesh being weak is actually a sympathetic one. In any
case he leaves them dozing and when necessary wakes them up
and includes them in the next conflict – facing the betraying kiss
of Judas.

So what are we watching for? In the old rigged ships of the
past a ship's night-watchman would shin up the mainsail to a
look-out basket known as the crow's nest. Every quarter of an
hour he would report 'all's well' to those on duty on the deck if
nothing had been sighted, but if he saw another vessel he would
shout 'ship a'hoy' and give the general compass direction.
Today it's done with the use of a radar scanner. If something is
noticed, the alarm is sounded and all hands are on 'red alert'.

Part of what it means to 'watch', I believe, is to scan everything new and weigh it against the Scriptures. As we listen to,
watch or read the news our spiritual antennae should alert us
to the need to pray. I often find myself praying then and there
for someone, some group of people or some leader as I am
alerted to different news items. When it comes to local news,
this kind of praying falls directly into the realms of hospitality,
for here, on our doorstep, are situations that we can bring
before the Lord, and in doing so we can include a readiness in

our praying to be prepared to be part of the answer. In other words, we are willing to contact by letter or phone or in person the one who has been tragically hurt, or bereaved, to offer support and friendship. It may be that the contact will have a totally different purpose, such as campaigning on behalf of something that is wrong. The point is that our cries heavenwards about our community are translated into something practical earthwards.

In a fast, computerised age when things that have been around for only a year or two are binned, there's a huge burden on Christian leaders to come up with something new to keep the attention of their congregations. That is relatively easy. What is harder is for the church to keep watch on developments that affect the everyday lives of people and maintain an effective voice that sounds the alert when standards and disciplines erode. The cultural shock for someone from the first century coming back to life and being thrust into the eighteenth century would not be that huge, even though 1,700 years had passed. Scientific advances would hold some interest. Social behaviour would be only slightly changed. But imagine showing someone around your neighbourhood who had come from the nineteenth century. The further advancement in those 100 or so years would totally bemuse him, and probably the most mind-boggling thing would be the speed and the breadth of discovery that had occurred, and the way social behaviour had adapted, often for the worse, to accommodate it all.

It is well known that every ground-breaking discovery for good has a flipside of abuse for evil.

It is well known that every ground-breaking discovery for good has a flipside of abuse for evil. Leonardo de Vinci always feared that his inventions might be used to harm. That was in the latter half of the fifteenth century and concerned a handful of drawings. Now, on every continent, innumerable inventions are springing up in order to make us more healthy, to help us to communicate more quickly and to enable us to fight crime locally, nationally and internationally more effectively. But every invention has the potential to work against us.

This is the environment we're living in, and watchfulness, alertness and great wisdom are needed by the church to sift through the new things that come to the surface, to see whether or not they can survive the scrutiny of the timeless word of God. The last 100 years has seen issues concerning the sanctity of life, such as abortion, frozen embryos, cloning, euthanasia, and then issues of sexual bias, alternative 'families', and drug use (to name a few) rise to the fore and have caused the church to search the Scriptures and fight for the faith in a way unknown in previous generations. For me, 'watching' involves keeping the mind alert so as not to give up the old and true because something new seems more attractive and modern or more acceptable in our society. The above are just some issues for us to watch for and pray about as we seek to be light in our communities.

Neighbourhood prayerwalking

Some people think you can only pray sitting down or on your knees or with your head bowed. Actually, there's no biblical reference to sitting or closing your eyes when you pray. References abound to standing, lying prostrate, lifting up your eyes, and praying at all times and in all places. Prayerwalking has become popular in recent years, though I believe it's a practice that has been done for centuries. Perhaps the new phenomenon is prayer-driving, which I do quite a bit, and you certainly have to keep your eyes open then! So what is prayerwalking all about? It sounds pretty heavy and intense.

When we have friends to stay we often go for a walk in the country and we talk as we walk. So walking and talking naturally go together. Prayerwalking is exactly what the words imply: praying while you are walking.

Some would find evidence for it when God told Joshua to go throughout the land, promising him every bit of land that the sole of his foot touched (Joshua 1:3). This may or may not be the case. I don't think specific biblical proof texts need to be found. We don't need proof texts for what comes naturally. God never intended us to separate the secular from the sacred, so to identify a place or position to pray as being correct or incorrect is missing the point. The Jews eventually became very prescriptive as to how people's relationship with God should be developed, but God was often blowing their theories (as he still does today). Jacob had to admit, 'Surely the Lord is in this place' (Genesis 28:16) when the place in question was an arbitrary resting place because he was tired from his journey. Yet here the Lord imparted one of history's most important promises. Adam, Cain, Noah, Abraham and Moses all discovered that God wanted to chat in places they would never have considered holy.

The Samaritan woman at Jacob's well, centuries later, would have been surprised that the traditional places of worship that she had mentioned (Jerusalem for the Jews, and 'this mountain' [Mount Gerazim] for the Samaritans) were swept away in favour of an 'anywhere/anyplace' teaching, as long as it was 'in Spirit and in truth' (John 4:24).

With this in mind, prayerwalking is a way in which we can talk to the Lord about our community as we walk through it. The most natural form of prayerwalking is when we pray as we are going about our everyday business, as we walk home after delivering the children to school, as we shop or take the dog for a walk. For here we pass establishments and ordinary homes that will benefit from our prayers as we ask the Lord to touch them supernaturally. We can pray that the love of the husband and wife in that house would be strong; pray that the parents would be good leaders of their children and a good example of fatherhood and motherhood; pray that the children would be obedient and grow to be godly people. This can be done while you drive from place to place too.

But we can be more organised than this. Groups of people often gather with the specific purpose of praying for various places in the community. We may, for example, pick a local business, organisation, hospital, school, police or fire station and pray that the working environment would be healthy, and that the welfare of the community, not selfish ambition, would be a motivator of all they do. Pray for any Christian Unions in the workplace, that they may be effective among their colleagues. In Jeremiah 29:7, the prophet challenges the people to seek the welfare or peace of the city where they live: 'Seek the peace and prosperity of the city to which I have carried you into exile. Pray to the Lord for it, because if it prospers, you too will prosper.' If we don't pray for our businesses, who will? If we don't pray for the companies for which we work, who will?

The most natural form of prayerwalking is when we pray as we are going about our everyday business.

Our schools need all the prayer backing they can get! Where there are Christian teachers, they may be the only representatives of Jesus that some students or parents will ever encounter. Let's pray they will have the patience, courage and strength to stand up for what's right. Hospitals and doctors' surgeries need our prayers too. The medical profession can be Christ's hands of mercy and tenderness, as well as healing. They need to know there is a greater power beyond their training and skill.

Let me identify three reasons to prayerwalk. First, vision. As we walk and pray, we learn to see our neighbours through God's eyes. We might even begin to sense who God is drawing to himself and we can become part of it. Second, relationship. As we pray for people's homes, and seek to develop our neighbourliness with them, we inevitably learn of specific things to pray for, and sometimes we can let them know that we are praying for those things and as a result the friendships deepen. Third, hope. As we pray for our community, we stop being negative about leaders, conditions and areas of concern, because we have focused on what God can do and that raises a level of hope for our cities.

Peter Wagner calls prayerwalking 'praying on site with insight'.[2] We gain this insight by the Holy Spirit, who gives us the initial and ongoing inspiration and guidance, and also by learning about the village, town or city. The history of the community, its famous and infamous historic events, uncovers items for prayer. Some information will cause us to thank the Lord for its heritage; other information will cause us to repent on behalf of the community, as Nehemiah did. Generational and cultural sins can deeply affect whole neighbourhoods. This is part of healing our land, and it will lay a foundation for hospitality to thrive where once separateness and an almost ritual individualism have existed.

PUTTING PRINCIPLES INTO PRACTICE

1. Following the pattern of one of Paul's prayers in the epistles, what specific things would you want to pray for your neighbours?

2. If Jesus appeared to you and said, 'Watch and pray,' what would you do differently about the things that concern you at the moment?

3. You may already be aware of Christians prayerwalking in your area, and you could join them. But if there's not something already established, why not begin to pray as you walk around your neighbourhood?

4. Read the following verses and note the things you can pray for those who do not yet know Jesus: John 6:44; John 16:8–9; 1 Timothy 2:1–4.

9

Strangers on our Shores

> Like you, I will remember that I grew up in the home of
> others, and in a foreign land I faced deadly dangers. So that,
> whoever asks my hospitality as you do now, I would not
> know how to turn away. In future you will stay here in safety,
> like me.
>
> (Theseus in 'Oedipus at Colon' by Sophocles)

If it is true that hospitality and friendship are essential to any
relationship with our neighbours, then to give hospitality to
foreign visitors, whom at one time we might have described as
strangers, seems an obvious focus if we live in an area where
such people are to be found. There are two categories of visitors from abroad that I wish to identify at this point: international students and asylum seekers. These people will come
chiefly from a totally different culture from ours, and that in
itself needs to be understood if we are to allow our hearts to
resonate with their feelings.

Understanding culture

Culture is something every people group creates for itself: it's
their way of living life; it's the way a certain group functions
and organises itself. It becomes their society. As children are
born into this social organisation, they learn the behaviour and
belief system that has been passed down through the generations. What they observe and learn from their fellow country-
men becomes the framework of their understanding about life
and gradually answers most of the questions they have about

the way they live. This process enables them to accept, adopt and make sense of their customs. Culture is the lifestyle of that group, and as such it is never individualistic.

Culture forms people's initial understanding, not only of their own existence, but of the whole world. It is usually grown out of repeated sayings and doings that over years mould inner attitudes and motivations, and finally mutate into a very complex system that is unique to that society. Over centuries and a wide range of civilisation on different continents, huge diversities in worldview have grown up. For instance, one of the foundational tensions for Christians in the West, as we've seen, is that the West's worldview is largely based on a Greek philosophy of life, which is vastly different from the Hebrew philosophy of life that we find in the Scriptures. The West likes to compartmentalise the physical and the spiritual, so it is not surprising to find that generally there are differences in value, worth and custom between the 'Western' and 'Middle-eastern' worldviews when it comes to the understanding of Scripture. To illustrate, consider the following general comparisons.

Western society is normally more individualistic, which is shown graphically in the elderly's desire to stay as independent as possible for as long as possible, whereas non-Western societies tend to be much more family orientated. In Western society, the elderly tend to be forgotten; in non-Western cultures the elderly are among the most respected. In Western society children are expected to leave home and become independent as soon as possible; in non-Western societies children mostly remain at home until they are married. In our Western society, the sexes have become more equal; in non-Western societies there is still a gulf between them and males are always more important. In business, Western society is performance-orientated; non-Western societies tend to be experience-orientated. Western societies run their lives by clocks and diaries; non-Western societies are not so time conscious. From a religious point of view, Western society is man-centered, religious experience is individualistic and sacred and secular are separated; the non-Western society is more God-centred, religious experiences are corporate and there's an integration between the sacred and the secular.

International students

The above, and other areas where cultures differ, can be seen as opportunities for conversation, and they highlight areas where help can be given. For instance, some visitors may not be used to the British climate, so help to find proper clothing might be appreciated. Obviously language can be a major obstacle, particularly slang and idioms, and provides an opportunity to help. Visitors might well be bewildered by such things as the balance of wealth. Some Western students will own as much as, or more than, the most wealthy from an Eastern or Middle-eastern country. In some instances Western students will come from families who earn a yearly income that could feed a whole village in the developing world.

Most international students expect cultural differences in major areas such as food or language, but there are differences in unexpected areas. For example, the way people interact with each other: how long a person looks at another person in the eye, how we show affection towards a member of the opposite sex, how much personal space is appropriate. I remember watching a speeded-up film of British and Japanese business delegates interacting at a conference; the British wanted to relate close up and the Japanese were desperately trying to create their own space. The result was that they moved around the hall, led by the Japanese in their search for more space, which was very funny at triple speed. If you say something that a Japanese person disagrees with they will smile and nod, which actually means 'no, no, no'. Their culture does not easily offer a way for them to oppose you face to face, so they will find a way to avoid offending you and also to avoid losing their cultural face. If you ask an Indian a direct question that

They will smile and nod, which actually means 'no, no, no'.

could be answered 'yes' or 'no', they will move their head from side to side with a slight nod, push out their lips slightly and have a twinkle in their eye as they do so. It means 'yes, if you like, and no, if you like'. If you want to discuss an issue with an Indian, don't ask a direct question, expecting a monosyllabic answer. If you offer hospitality to an Indian it will quite often be declined. Don't be put off by this; it is part of their culture and it happens even among their own families, so persevere.

As in all life scenarios, it is the unexpected that can bring disorientation. It is when someone is not expecting a difference that the difference can be dramatic. Westerners, to our shame, are generally not good at adapting to others, especially non-Westerners. We have a tendency to be proud and aloof. Because we speak the trade language of the world, we make little attempt to learn even basic phrases in the languages of places we visit, and, for the most part, we show little interest in the different nuances of other languages or cultures. Someone once asked: if a person who speaks many languages is a multilinguist and a person who speaks two languages is a bilinguist, what do we call someone who speaks just one? The answer, of course, is British! We also have the annoying tendency to consider other cultures as more primitive than our own. But it's not a matter of being better or worse; it's simply different. As we learn about the differences, we'll be in a better position to help our visiting students fit into our culture during their time here.

If we were to visit international students in their student accommodation we would learn a great deal simply by observing the objects in their room. We might see a prayer rug, an icon, a mezuzah (a Hebrew scroll mounted on the door frame) or a family god on a shelf. These will indicate to us something about what is important to them.

Every year new students come from all corners of the world to study at our universities and colleges. There are many reasons for doing so, which include the belief that we can offer them better teaching and facilities than their own country or that to study in a different culture will enhance their education.

Whatever the reason, certain facts are always present: when they first arrive they are lonely, disorientated and often homesick. Many of us remember those feelings to a lesser degree during our own first few days at university or college. Add to that an unfamiliar culture, language and climate, and we might begin to understand the issues facing these students.

Here are ready-made opportunities for hospitality in towns and cities where international students reside – opportunities to demonstrate to them that we are aware they exist, aware of their need for friendship and aware that they need acceptance. Some churches already operate hospitality by finding ways to introduce Christian students to a church, and they encourage their members to invite students for meals. It is true that all students can do with this kind of hospitality, not just international ones, for most students study away from home. But I want to explore the possibilities of spreading the net wider so that we don't just invite those from another part of the UK. We need to think particularly about those who will feel the most lonely and disorientated. For example, international students almost always need some help with how to do basic things. It is easy to make simple but catastrophic mistakes. When I was at Bible college my wife and I befriended a Jamaican student who had come over here with his wife while he studied for the ministry. He had been married for just two years, and therefore felt it was right for them both to come. His wife had managed to get a job over here as a nurse so that she could support him as he studied for the pastorate. But there was one problem. Before arriving here the only map they had had of Great Britain was a tiny one in the back of a diary. As we sat eating lunch together on Christmas Day it was now with some laughter that he explained the reason why his wife had gone for a job in Glasgow while he was in London: Glasgow, Manchester and London were the only places marked on the map, and they didn't seem that far apart! When they had arrived the previous September and discovered their blunder there was no laughter – only despair, self-recrimination and a total sense of lostness and failure. It was the practical care and hospitality of the Christian community that not only saved the day for this student, but also enabled him, three months later, to laugh about it.

It is a vision of the Lord Jesus and his love for international students that will enable us to offer hospitality and help prevent the common feelings of loneliness, confusion, various kinds of pressure and frustration. International students enter this country with a mix of strong, close-knit, unhappy or tense family or community backgrounds. The loneliness they feel forces them to seek friendship with whoever will befriend them. Sometimes that will spell trouble for them, but they do it anyway because there is a huge hole in their hearts. They miss the noise of babies and children from their inner family circles and they especially miss the older relatives who give wisdom and stability to their family group. As you build relationships with them, ask about family members. If they are happy to talk about it, ask often, especially if there's an ongoing situation that concerns them. International students come to our universities and colleges expecting to build a new circle of friends and they don't expect the sudden isolation that so often shatters their dreams. As I write this page I have learned that an international student has committed suicide in the hall of residence where my eldest daughter is at university. Sadly this is not a rare occurrence at our universities.

The pressure to adapt to this culture and yet retain their own cultural identity is keenly felt.

The pressures on students are immense, as they are caught between cultures. The pressure to adapt to this culture and yet retain their own cultural identity is keenly felt. They will learn to eat our food, wear our clothes, listen to our music, but they don't want to fit in to all of our ways. The options are simple: either they have to adapt without integrating entirely or not adapt and be lonely.

Then there's the pressure to succeed after making the trip over here. They feel they owe it to their families back home to do well. Yet to do that they have to master the language, and to master it they must study harder than most indigenous students. That pressure also limits the time they have to adapt to the new culture. They get very tired because they have to listen more carefully than others to lectures in a language not their own. They even get tired in a conversation because, until they are really fluent with English, they are having to translate as they go along. Those who have open hearts can alleviate all of these pressures and needs. Numerous opportunities are there, and if we're caring and sensitive to their culture, there is a harvest waiting to be reaped.

My wife and I once gave some hospitality to a Bible student from Romania, who said he thought he would have to return to his home country without experiencing English hospitality after four or more years in England. We would do well to consider the value and impact of an invitation to our home for the weekend or an occasional meal or a stay for part of a vacation. William Woodward, a retired missionary to Japan, says:

> The Japanese, in their professions, businesses and education, are notoriously indifferent to formal religion but . . . they have a deep respect for people who live their religion . . . it is the shame of western Christianity that, while much effort is made to spread the Gospel in Japan, very little is done in the west to enable Japanese visitors or residents to hear and understand the Gospel of Jesus Christ . . . the answer is for Americans and other western peoples to open up their churches, homes and hearts to the stranger in their midst . . . The front door of every Christian home in the west is a battleline of Christendom and a gateway to the evangelization of Japan. Each door should be open inward in welcome and outward in Christian witness and service.[1]

John Haggai of the Haggai Institute, whose philosophy was to train international Bible teachers to go back and make a difference in their own countries, once told me that our approach to international students may have far-reaching effects: 'Who knows what it will accomplish? It may influence some future government minister, and thus our Christian values might make a difference in politics or social justice.' Welcoming international students into our homes and churches is one way of fulfilling the Great Commission in other parts of the world without ever leaving our homeland.

Catherine Weston writes: 'Helping international student ministry grow in your church will mean establishing a core group of committed people who will pray and work together.'[2] It is wise first to plan an introductory meeting for any within the church who have an interest in this ministry. Ensure that the leadership and any missionary committee know what you are planning and are invited. Hopefully this will immediately attract those with a heart for hospitality, those who have experience of working abroad or those who have international colleagues in the workplace. Not all who come will become part of the core group that will do most of the work, but some will be happy to be called upon for specific events.

Making contact

Ron and Patty McCulloch, who work for the Christian organisation Friends International, have been helpful in passing on some very useful information. Friends International has staff in many centres in the UK. Direct contact can be made with a worker in quite a few areas. If you have access to a computer, you can see if your area has a worker by logging on to www.friendsinternational.org.uk or telephoning their headquarters on 020 8780 3511.

Some universities run a hospitality scheme for international students. Church members would, in some cases, be able to make contact with the relevant office, often the international student advisor or officer. In addition, some universities have an international student chaplain.

The national scheme HOST is advertised in universities. The initiative involves internationals in one town being linked with a host in another part of the UK. This would ordinarily mean an invitation to spend a few days with their host, possibly around Christmas or Easter. Although this is not a Christian organisation, it is good for Christians to get themselves onto the list of hosts. There are regional co-ordinators of the scheme. See www.hostuk.org or telephone 020 7254 3039. There are similar schemes in most countries.

The Jehovah's Witnesses make contact with students from mainland China by meeting them at key places like Chinatown in Birmingham, where they just start chatting to them. Mainstream churches could easily adopt a similar practice. Or why not endeavour to engage them in conversation in shopping queues, at the school gates (where holiday jobs as au pairs often take them), or on public transport? Many international students will respond positively to an individual taking a genuine interest in them or offering practical help to them. We need to overcome our inbuilt British reserve in situations like this and not wait to be introduced. We can also take the initiative in visiting internationals if they are moving into a house in our area. It's a good opportunity to extend a warm welcome to them.

Max Kershaw, who spent many years working among Muslim students on both sides of the Atlantic, noted that many of them have the idea that Westerners are 'superficial in their friendships and not particularly willing to open their hearts, homes, and kitchens to foreigners'.[3] Kershaw suggests that conversation is vital and in engaging them in discussion we may not agree with what they say, and may even want to argue, but we should not feel compelled to win every argument. 'In the Arab world,' he says, 'disagreements are often a way friendships are tested.'[4] (It should be noted, however, that whereas Jews and Arabs generally like a good argument, that is not true of all cultures.)

Kershaw goes on to explain that in extending hospitality we must be careful to offer only food and drink that is acceptable to our guest. It has been mentioned before that an open heart, which is the forerunner to an open home, requires us to think ourselves into our guest's world. Therefore, to consider whether certain food would be off the menu is a courtesy we can't ignore. It is not courteous, polite or considerate to have the attitude

(however well intentioned) that they are now in our country
and should therefore expect to eat what we eat. It runs deeper
than that, especially where Jews and Muslims are involved. On
the other hand, if you have invited an international guest to
your home, having considered what foods might be off limits for
them, let them taste a typical British meal. That, says Ron and
Patty McCulloch, is better than trying to 'cook a curry for
Indians and stir-fry for Chinese, unless you really know your
spices'.[5]

I remember sharing a service with a young Jewish man who
had come to know Jesus as his Messiah and we were invited
back to someone's house for a barbecue. As we queued for our
meal the host said, 'We only have pork sausages. Is that OK?'
Great embarrassment was saved as my friend revealed that
though he was Jewish he hadn't followed kosher requirements
for some time. But it highlights the need to think ourselves into
others' shoes. Don't assume all messianic Jews have jettisoned
kosher requirements just because they have made a commitment to Jesus.

We must also be discreet in our male–female relationships in
our guest's presence, and particularly any opposite sex interaction with guests, for among most Muslims, friendships are
formed only between those of the same sex. They misinterpret
the openness of Western women, thinking that it means a possible intimate relationship with them.

Times of need or vulnerability

Be especially aware of times of vulnerability. It may be an accident or death in the family, or the news of political unrest in
their country when they are far from family and friends to fully
identify with the crisis their loved ones are facing. It may be cultural or religious feasts that they are missing for the first time
because they have not yet discovered other nationals to share in
them. We have discovered that this vulnerability also creates a
hunger to discover the cultural and religious practices of
Britain (with sensitive and winsome testimony).

Christmas and Easter holidays are particularly good opportunities to invite international students to come to your home or a church event. Often the break isn't long enough to return home, or if it is they can't afford to do so.

Ron and Patty McCulloch mention other things in offering hospitality to foreign students in their leaflet *Hints for Hosts*, including informing your guest that you have a pet cat or dog, being unaware that the British enthusiasm for walking in the rain across muddy fields is not shared by others, and that if your hospitality is reciprocated do accept, remembering that you may need to take off your shoes.

Asylum seekers

If we take asylum seekers out of the political arena, where they have become simply objects of political power and control, and instead position them in the context of the Judeo/Christian call to be hospitable to the stranger in the land, then the issues become clearer. When we consider that the Jesus of history has come among us dressed as a gardener and a walking companion to the disappointed and the downcast, and he claims to be there among us today as the naked, the hungry, the thirsty and the incorrectly imprisoned, and he demonstrates a love that changes inaccurately held views of society, then we, as his disciples, see clearer

While the politics goes on, they stand on our soil, needy and disorientated.

that we have a responsibility to reach out and help. At a forum on refugees and asylum seekers at Montmorency Uniting Church in the USA, the Revd David Pargeter, of the church's Justice and International Mission Unit, said this:

> Strangeness always generates tension. What is new and unusual always stimulates some kind of unease. Sometimes it's excitement and anticipation. Sometimes it is fear and apprehension. So it could be said that we end up with either xenophobia or xenophilia (fear

of the stranger or love of the stranger). I want to suggest to you that this tension is overcome by the universally possible and the universally transforming practice of hospitality. Hospitality turns aliens into friends. Hospitality is a much better way of dealing with strangers.[6]

Deuteronomy 10:19 – 'you are to love those who are aliens' – implies a perspective on the immigration process whereby we see Christ in the ones who stand and knock at the door of our nation. You don't have to enter the politics of it if you don't want to, but the fact is that while the politics goes on, they stand on our soil, needy and disorientated. Jonathan Sacks, the UK Chief Rabbi, has written:

> The Hebrew Bible contains the great command, 'you shall love your neighbour as yourself' (Leviticus 19:18) and this has been taken as the basis of biblical morality. But it is not; it is only part of it. Jewish sages have noted that on only one occasion does the Hebrew Bible command us to love our neighbour, but in 37 places it commands us to love the stranger; our neighbour is one we love because he is like ourselves. The stranger is one we are taught to love precisely because he is not like ourselves.[7]

George Carey, the former Archbishop of Canterbury, also addressed this important issue of hospitality. In his Christmas Day 2000 sermon he said:

> Luke makes a point of saying that 'there was no room' for the family of Jesus except in the animal enclosure adjoining the local hostelry. Is it not astonishing – and yet all too believable – that even the sight of a young woman going into labour could not unlock a response of generous hospitality? Fear with its sister insecurity shuts doors and refuses to allow the stranger in.
>
> Just a week ago I visited a temporary shelter run by St Mungo's, the largest agency in London for homeless people. A senior member of staff repeated the all too familiar story that while everyone wants the homeless to have a roof over their heads they always want it in someone else's street or another neighbourhood. Our instinct to do

what is right clashes with another instinct – NIMBY: 'not in my back yard' . . . Of course, such things are rarely simple. They only seem so to those who are not involved in the local issues. We know that from our situation in east Kent. As hundreds of asylum seekers pour through Dover weekly, local people find it difficult to reconcile the duty of hospitality which has been so characteristic of our nation for many years, with the prospect of finite resources being over-burdened by the sheer numbers of new arrivals. It is to the credit of the people of the ports of east Kent that resentment has not totally blocked the spirit of human kindness and hospitality.[8]

Migration, travelling in search of one's true home, even travelling to find answers to life, as well as the whole idea of life being a journey, are familiar metaphors in the Scriptures and later church history. During the sixteenth century, there were large numbers of Protestant refugees fleeing persecution, and as a result there was a 'significant resurgence of the moral credibility and practical relevence of hospitality to needy strangers. Welcoming these persons, Calvin asserted, was the most "sacred" kind of hospitality.'[9] In all these, hospitality features as a key ingredient. 'When an alien lives with you in your land, do not ill-treat him . . . [he] must be treated as one of your native-born. Love him as yourself, for you were aliens in Egypt' (Leviticus 19:33–34).

Jesus' own life consisted of travelling and a need to find hospitality. There was the 'no room in the inn' event at his birth of course, and Matthew's Gospel tells of the whole family's urgent flight into Egypt to escape the tyrant Herod. In adult life, Jesus knew a degree of homelessness, and himself said, 'Foxes have holes and birds of the air have nests, but the Son of Man has nowhere to lay his head' (Luke 9:58).

The plight of asylum seekers in the UK has been a growing and sometimes emotive issue since the Immigration and Asylum Bill began its journey through parliament in 1999, to become law in 2000.

UK facts and figures[10]

In 2002, there were just under 86,000 asylum applications to the UK. This figure excludes dependants. With dependants, the figure is 111,000 and 41 per cent of these were granted refugee status. The Refugee Council estimates that at least 54 per cent of asylum seekers are successful at some stage of the asylum process. On 30th March 2003, there were 20,600 applications awaiting initial decision of which the largest proportion was from Iraq, Zimbabwe and Afghanistan, and 1,355 asylum seekers were detained in prisons around the UK, of which 91 per cent were male. The average age of asylum seekers is 27 years and 80 per cent are male.

The UK currently has more applications for asylum than any other country in Europe in terms of numbers (until recently, Germany topped this list). However, in terms of the number of asylum seekers in relation to a country's wealth, the UK ranks only sixth in Europe and seventy-eighth in the world. In terms of numbers of asylum seekers per head of the population, the UK ranks only eighth in Europe (2000), after Belgium, Ireland, the Netherlands, Austria, Denmark, Sweden and Luxembourg.

Nationalities

The vast majority of asylum seekers continue to come from Afghanistan, Iraq, Somalia and Sri Lanka, where there are well-known civil and other wars. Other countries include China, Columbia, Ecuador, Iran, Turkey, Pakistan, the Federal Republic of Yugoslavia and Zimbabwe. The countries from which considerably more asylum seekers have come since 2000 are Iraq, Afghanistan, Angola, the Democratic Republic of Congo (formerly Zaire), Ethiopia, Sierra Leone, Somalia, Tanzania and Zimbabwe.

Refugees

According to the United Nations High Commission for Refugees, there were an estimated 169,354 refugees living in Britain in March 2002. Refugees are people who have been given this special status by the country in which they have sought asylum. The number of refugees in Britain represents just over 1 per cent of the total world population of refugees. They have UN travel documents and the same basic rights to travel freely and access services as other UK citizens. For these reasons, their precise numbers are not recorded or known.

Asylum seekers and issues of criminality

It is widely accepted that asylum seekers may well be victims of crime and injustice, including racism. However, there are also other links between some asylum seekers and crime. Crucially, it needs to be understood that there is no way an asylum seeker can come to this country without committing an offence! Most come from countries where they have to get a visa to travel, as they cannot leave their countries without this (also airlines will not accept passengers without the appropriate visa). Naturally, there is no special asylum visa, so most will acquire false documents, which ultimately means involving people traffickers. Though the government is making it very difficult for so-called 'bogus' asylum seekers to come in, they have made it equally difficult for genuine asylum seekers to come. Again, this may change under new legislation, where it is anticipated that people can seek asylum in a country near to them. But it still will not be that easy, as they will need documents to leave their own country. If they are in fear of persecution, they are not going to approach the authorities to ask for documents and so put their lives at further risk.

Many only claim asylum when they are discovered. Others may overstay on a visitor's visa, give false information in order to gain permission to enter the UK, or are in possession of false documents and only claim asylum once their misdemeanours have been discovered.

Others come from societies where there are high levels of violent crime and, in some cases, a tradition of blood feuds. I've already mentioned involvement with people traffickers, but some are involved with people smugglers. People traffickers are

individuals or groups who con people into a system of illegal
employment and who themselves profit from the illegal work,
whereas people smugglers are individuals or groups with an
organised supply of people who already want to enter another
country, and the smuggling of other goods often accompanies
their illegitimate activity. The United
Nations Declaration of Human Rights
states that everyone has the right to seek
asylum and freedom away from persecution. The term 'asylum seeker' refers to
someone who believes they are in serious
danger at home from war, famine, political persecution or natural disaster.

Everyone has the right to seek asylum and freedom away from persecution.

Asylum seekers are granted residency in Britain if they meet
criteria laid down in the 1951 UN Convention. This states that
they must have a 'well-founded fear of persecution' on the
grounds of 'race, religion, nationality, membership of a particular social group or political opinion'. If these criteria are not
applicable but the Home Office still believes that the asylum
seeker would face danger if they returned to their country of
origin, the person may be granted 'exceptional leave to remain'.
This means they can remain in the UK, usually for a period
of four years. After this, they can apply for leave to remain
permanently.

Most asylum seekers are given temporary admission, enabling them to live freely in the UK provided that they live at a
certain address and report to a police station or immigration
officer either weekly or monthly. Since April 2000, the National
Asylum Support Service (NASS), a division of the Home
Office, is responsible for providing asylum seekers with accommodation and the means to cover their basic needs. Asylum
seekers in need of accommodation are dispersed to one of the
country's 'cluster regions'. They have no choice as to where they
are sent. All the cluster areas are outside London and the South
East and the chief reason for dispersing people is to relieve
these areas of some of the responsibility and expense of

meeting asylum seekers' needs. The Home Office states: 'Asylum seekers will be housed in areas that are suitable for them. This takes into account . . . existing multicultural communities, appropriate housing and the scope to develop voluntary and community sector support.'

A new Nationality, Immigration and Asylum Act 2002 came into force on 8th January 2003. This states that any asylum seeker who asks for asylum after having entered the country (i.e. did not seek asylum at the port of entry) and does not have dependants will not be entitled to any financial help. This will mean that we will be back to the situation of 1996, where there were a lot of starving homeless single asylum seekers on the streets, and voluntary organisations, including churches, will have far more demands placed on their resources and willingness to show hospitality.

In order to put ourselves into the shoes of these people, we have to imagine what it is like to flee your own country and leave everything behind: your family and friends, your hopes and dreams – in fact everything that speaks of a normal existence in the country you know so well. Faced with these prospects, there is only the tentative hope that somehow life will be better in a new country and that you will be safe and able to rebuild your life. But first you have to overcome the immediate suspicion, even hostility, you are met with.

Even if we give a lot of time to thinking and praying about their plight, are we really open to being part of the answers to our thoughts and prayers? One couple known to me (I will call them Tom and Anne) often expressed all the feelings that good Christian people do towards them, and then one day those feelings were suddenly put on the spot when a local newspaper article attracted their attention:

Foster carers required to look after young people who seek asylum in the UK and come to this country without their parents. The majority of these young people will be male and come from Kosovo or Afghanistan. If you feel you have the qualities to care for traumatised young people who have to live in a country that will be strange to them we would like to hear from you. You will need to have time and space for these young people and at least one spare room in your house, an enlightened approach to the position of children who seek asylum and a strong sympathy with their position.

This normal Christian couple shared the thoughts and feelings of many of us prior to this event:

My home is important to me. It is my private place where I can shut the door on the world. My house is my security, I feel safe behind the Yale and the UPVC windows. It is my future, my financial comfort, it will increase in value. Most of all, it is mine (mortgage notwithstanding). I am king. Yet traditional Christian teaching tells me that these things are transient and that my house is not mine at all – I am just a custodian for my short life span. I am to use this house in Christian service, to the glory of God. Of course we are happy to hold Bible studies, prayer meetings and young people's groups any time. We can always video our favourite TV programme if that is a problem. If God wanted us to do something very different, then he would see to it that we got a very different (i.e. bigger) house.

Along with these thoughts, which I suspect resonate with many of us, there were real heart-felt and empathic emotions going on. Tom continues:

I have long held a deep and genuine concern for the poor, lost and oppressed; for those who do not have the good fortune to be born into cosy, comfortable, insulated Great Britain. My Christian response has been to give, occasionally, to the aid agencies, and actively promote them in the church. I even went on a field trip to an African village to try and help. And of course I have prayed – prayed that God, in his mercy, would bring relief to the poor, freedom to the oppressed and justice to the afflicted. (How that was to be achieved must remain God's problem.) I remember one Sunday morning prattling in front of our church about asylum seekers – about how misunderstood they are, more often the victims than perpetrators, and too often dismissed as spongers off 'our' country. But our Christian response should be one of welcoming and embracing. They are God's creation just as much as we are, and anyway, this is not 'our' country; we just happen to live here for the moment. I felt really good about that and believed I had been an important witness to our church on a burning issue of the day. (Of course, it did not make the slightest difference to a single asylum seeker anywhere.)

Tom, according to Anne, had felt quite strongly that asylum seekers were 'aliens at the gates' and that as Christians we should be welcoming them. Her own thoughts will also beat in harmony with the thinking of many Christians in our land:

I had never met an asylum seeker. They were 'alien' to my thoughts, lifestyle and experience. I had at the same time been challenged over a period of two to three years by my lifestyle. I had been blessed with so much materially and had three healthy loving children, two of whom were married. What was my response? Isaiah 58:10 challenged me: 'If you spend yourselves on behalf of the hungry and satisfy the needs of the oppressed, then your light will rise in the darkness, and your night will become like the noonday.' I was perturbed and disquieted during this time that my light as a Christian did not shine. I wanted to do something meaningful, so I prayed. God always answers our prayers, and we saw the advertisement in the local paper. I sensed God speaking to us. I have to say that although I considered fostering children when my children were young, I had not visited those thoughts recently and I had certainly never imagined having teenage boys. Although I was very apprehensive and scared, I had peace and an excitement that I knew was from God.

One of the things that may well put people off fostering or adopting is the 'red tape': the long, often thought unnecessary drawn-out interviews that dig deep into our lives, and we wonder whether, having laid bare our hearts, we will have passed the test. If we don't, a whole lot of people know intimate details about us and we are left feeling that despite a sense of divine calling and desire to do what is right, we have been found not suitable. Inevitably the process has to take place and I can only encourage others to press on for what they believe is right. After all, in every birthing process there are pains. We ourselves have two adopted children and despite 'red tape' tensions we, in our own way, have shared the normal experiences, the joys of delivery outweighing the pains of the birthing process. Concerning their experiences Anne writes:

> The vetting process took several months and we eventually welcomed two lovely boys, aged 14 and 15, into our home in September 2001. They came with all their worldly possessions: one small bag between them and a basketball. There are so many joys that God gives you when you step out in faith, and one of them was when we took them to buy new trainers. The look on their faces as they tried them on was pure joy. Another amazing day was when one of them had a birthday; he had never had a birthday party and presents before.

All of life has its highs and lows and if we are wise we learn from both. Opening up your home to strangers is inevitably going to have its range of experiences. Anne says that there were some hard times too, in which they learned more about the real needs:

> I felt I was giving them everything in order that they would be really happy. I was giving them love, security, material possessions and a comfortable way of life. But over the months I realised that this was not what they wanted. Although they did not have a problem with us as a family, they actually did not want foster care. They wanted to live independently with people from their own country and culture. On many occasions this made me feel rejected, but it also made me think very hard about how I so often reject God in the good things he has to offer me day by day. How must God feel?
>
> Another difficulty we had to overcome was the attitude of others to asylum seekers. We constantly reminded ourselves (and others) that the teenagers we had in our home were victims. They were the

oppressed, and although we could not change the world we could influence the lives of these two young people. The difficulties weren't just on our side, obviously. One of the boys who came to us initially had had bad experiences of living with his family in his country and this was one of the main reasons for seeking asylum. He found it very difficult to live in a family situation in which love and care for each other was expressed.

Anne notes that the song by Graham Kendrick that begins 'For the joys and for the sorrows, the best and worst of times, for this we have Jesus' (1994, Make Way Music) encapsulates their experiences, and without the help of Jesus they would not be able to continue. Such a sentiment reverberates through all our evangelism because Jesus himself admitted that he would send

In every birthing process there are pains.

us out like sheep among a pack of wolves. But it is precisely this experience of needing the help of Jesus and the power of the Holy Spirit that ensures spiritual growth in our lives.

There are other things to learn when we engage in hospitality among foreigners, whether they are asylum seekers or international students or settled neighbours. We learn about their worldview and how sometimes it echoes the Scriptures in a way our worldview doesn't, even when it is superimposed by Christian thinking. Anne writes that her asylum boys taught her a lot about sharing: 'They said that if they had a pig they killed it, cooked it, ate it and shared it with their neighbours and none of it was saved for another day' (see Luke 12:22–34). She says that they've learned what a blessing it is to be born in a wealthy country and to share this with those who do not have. She has begun to realise what it means when Jesus says, 'It is easier for a camel to go through the eye of a needle than for a rich man to enter the kingdom of God' (Matthew 19:24).

We all know that it is relatively easy to give to Tearfund and then indulge ourselves at Christmas and not feel too guilty. Tom and Anne have been personally challenged since fostering asylum seekers and Anne admits that before they came she was scared that she would not like them. She feared that they would be noisy, intrusive, smelly and demanding, and her time would not be her own. Having prayed that God would help her to like them, he helped her not only to like them, but to love them. She says: 'I often wonder what Jesus will say to me when I enter heaven. What might he say to you? Will he say to me: "Why did you have all those clothes stored in your wardrobe when so many of my children are naked?" Will he say: "Why did you store food in your cupboard when most of my children were hungry?"'

For Tom and Anne, like many of us, awareness of the plight of asylum seekers was always there. It sometimes compels us to give to the relevant charities, sometimes to pray for those who work with them and seek a better life for them. But for this couple, at least, God was requiring more. Maybe he's asking that of you too. Tom recalls: 'Suddenly, praying and giving was not enough. We had to live it as well.'

The growth and dispersal of asylum seekers has created tremendous opportunities for churches in the UK to minister to people from many different lands, especially countries closed to the gospel. Many of us now find that some of these are living in our neighbourhood. Gradually, churches are responding to this challenge. Tearfund has an active ministry co-ordinating this and supporting churches across the UK in their work with asylum seekers. The World Evangelical Alliance is also actively involved in setting up a network of churches and Christian organisations involved in working with refugees across the whole world.

PUTTING PRINCIPLES INTO PRACTICE

1. Give some ideas as to how you would start talking with a stranger about the gospel.
2. Where are the most common gathering places for those from a different cultural or ethnic background near you?
3. In Acts 17 Paul is witnessing to some Greeks in Athens, and

apart from the Scriptures he also quotes Greek poetry. What books, songs or TV programmes might you use constructively in witnessing to others?

4. Imagine that you were communicating aspects of the British culture to a foreign student. List the top five cultural characteristics you would choose.

5. The sale board next door has come down and your new neighbours come from Afghanistan. Describe your feelings about this, the steps you would take to make them welcome and what difficulties you would expect to encounter.

6. If you live in a university town or city, or where there's a college or hospital campus, what practical steps could you, or your group, take to make contact with a foreign student? Is this something your church might consider as an outreach project?

10

Entertaining Angels

A ministering angel shall my sister be.
(Shakespeare, *Hamlet*, Act V scene 1)

Abraham is a model host for the three visitors who come to him 'by the oaks of Mamre'. It was at Mamre where Abraham and his nephew, Lot, famously separated (Genesis 13:18). Abraham had given his nephew the first choice of the land and, as Lot looked towards the horizon, the well-watered region of the valley of Sodom inspired him. He chose what he could 'see', unaware of how the people of Sodom really were (Genesis 13:13).

Abraham begins by offering the visitors a warm welcome:

Abraham . . . hurried from the entrance of his tent to meet them and bowed low to the ground. He said, 'If I have found favour in your eyes, my lord, do not pass your servant by. Let a little water be brought, and then you may all wash your feet and rest under this tree. Let me get you something to eat, so you can be refreshed and then go on your way – now that you have come to your servant.' 'Very well,' they answered, 'do as you say.' (Genesis 18:2–5).

The scene opens by revealing the identity of these dinner guests. Abraham, it appears, catches sight of some figures heading his way through the shimmering heat of the desert sun. What he sees, from a human perspective, is three 'men'. He would have seen such sights many times, but this day things are different.

144

On this particular day, Abraham and his wife are to experience a divine visitation. The Lord is visiting Abraham, but in human form, so that he might speak to him without overwhelming him.

There's another reason why God would appear in a 'theophany' like this. There is always the possibility of behaving unnaturally in the presence of someone whom we would rightly worship. If the Queen were coming for dinner, we would tend to behave unusually, or even unnaturally well. Yet there may also be a tendency to 'fumble' and something of our real selves might be hidden. But when a stranger comes for dinner, we behave more naturally and tend to be unhindered, so our normal character is revealed.

The three men appear during the hottest time of the day, when it was usual to rest. Abraham is probably already dozing off in a chair at the entrance to his tent when through his bleary eyes he makes out the familiar dust trail of travellers on the horizon. Immediately he shifts into high gear and becomes a model of true hospitality. He runs out to them as if they are long-lost relatives and greets them like royalty. He addresses the leader as 'my lord' (though some versions have the plural 'lords'). This is a title he also uses to address his God. The verb 'to bow down' is the appropriate posture for welcoming guests in the Middle East. It is also used many times to describe the posture in worshipping God (Genesis 24:26).

Abraham is clearly concerned that his apparent unreadiness for visitors might mean that they will bypass his home and travel on to the next one. He follows this display of warmth and respect by extending an invitation to quench their thirst and eat, saying that it will be his privilege to serve. If they will accept, the words imply, it will make his day.

The menu, Abraham indicates, will be modest and the accommodation humble; there's water to drink and to wash their weary, dusty feet. Sarah will quickly bake some bread and the tree will serve as a canopy for shade. The visitors are not going to stay long, but it will be long enough for Abraham and

Sarah to refresh them. Following his invitation, Abraham awaits their answer. Will they allow him the supreme honour of serving them? Will they stay? Their answer is brief (just four staccato words in Hebrew): 'Very well, do as you say.' Permission is granted.

Abraham hurries into the tent to Sarah.

> 'Quick,' he said, 'get three seahs of fine flour and knead it and bake some bread.' Then he ran to the herd and selected a choice, tender calf and gave it to a servant, who hurried to prepare it. He then brought some curds and milk and the calf that had been prepared, and set these before them. While they ate, he stood near them under a tree (18:6–8).

We can't help but sense Abraham's urgency. He hurries everywhere and tells everyone else to hurry. Sarah and then a young servant join the flurry of preparations. The verb 'take', used as a command, appears four times in rapid succession, giving the feeling that things are being prepared at a feverish pace. His generosity and the feeling of urgency are indications that Abraham regards this kind of hospitality as something that deserves the highest standard. At first glance the hospitality seems basic, but it is actually very generous: Sarah is to take three measures (seahs) of fine flour. The Old Testament scholar, Roland de Vaux, notes that a 'seah' is about eight litres[1] – so three seahs of best wheat flour would make a great quantity of bread, while to kill 'a choice, tender calf' for just three visitors shows real generosity, as a lamb or a goat would have been more than adequate (2 Samuel 12:4; Luke 15:27–30).

The guests arrive unannounced, at the worst possible time of day.

Abraham models true hospitality. Notice that this event was neither planned nor convenient. The guests arrive unannounced, at the worst possible time of day, when the kitchen is shut down and nothing is readily available. Abraham, though, serves with humility. He is secure in who he is. Having been blessed by God, he is free to serve others as if they are his only way of repaying the generosity he himself has received. He treats these men as if, for this one moment, they are the centre of his universe. He draws his whole family in and sets his household working. He handpicks the best of what he has and gives meticulous care to its preparation and presentation.

To dig a little deeper, considering a more devotional view of this passage, midday, being the hottest time, is symbolic of all those times when we get hot and bothered, anxious, wound up; in short – we need to rest. Unfortunately, we are so unused to resting and taking time out today that we confuse rest with inactivity. For when we finally get round to resting, it's because our bodies will no longer act. God never intended it to be that way. He didn't tell us to rest when our bodies couldn't cope any longer. He told us to rest frequently, one day in seven. And that rest was not inactivity – it was to feed on him. Just as the shepherd 'makes' his sheep 'lie down in green pastures' (Psalm 23:2) at the hottest time of the day (Song of Songs 1:7) so that they can feed, so we need to feed on him.

It is in the 'hot times', when the pressure is on, that a lack of rest leads us to do things out of character, simply because we have not taken time out and fed on God and his word. We often get to hear about the mitigating circumstances from defence lawyers as to the defendant's single slip from an otherwise exemplary life: it was the pressure at work, at home, in the marriage that made him go to pieces. The truth is that these pressures would not exist if we followed the Maker's instructions.

Abraham and Sarah were going through their own 'hot' patch. There wasn't a gynaecologist alive then or now who would have given them any hope for natural childbirth at their age. For Sarah it was a great disappointment and a stigma. For Abraham it was a confusion to be sorted: a promise of God that he would be the father of many nations and yet he was married to a woman who was barren. There might have been hope but for the fact that they'd already celebrated their diamond wedding anniversary. You tell me that's not pressure!

But God wants to refresh us. He wants to give us hope. All he requires is obedience to his ways. And Abraham, through his hospitality, is obedient to God's command about treatment given to strangers who come across his path.

What is even more fascinating is the very thing that Abraham doesn't realise. In treating strangers like royalty, he is in fact entertaining angels, and God himself. This is why Christians are exhorted to be hospitable to strangers (Hebrews 13:2). Such hospitality could welcome God right to the very core of our lives.

Many will have travelled to countries with far fewer resources than our own and will have experienced a form of hospitality not unlike Abraham's. Such occasions are unforgettable and you know that they carry God's stamp of approval and somehow it's as if God himself is looking after you. The early Christians saw this kind of hospitality not just as the fulfilment of ancient biblical law, but also as a primary method of evangelism.

In treating strangers like royalty, he is in fact entertaining angels, and God himself.

The great value of hospitality is the relationships that are made through talking, listening and feeling. This is often begun alongside the secondary occupation of eating, which is a mutual and necessary activity that is viewed as a gift by the visitor and an honourable service by the host. It is in the process of such relationship-building that Abraham discovers the purpose of this mysterious visit:

Then the Lord said, 'I will surely return to you about this time next year, and Sarah your wife will have a son.' Now Sarah was listening at the entrance to the tent, which was behind him. Abraham and Sarah were already old and well advanced in years, and Sarah was past the age of childbearing. So Sarah laughed to herself as she thought, 'After I am worn out and my master is old, will I now have this pleasure?' Then the Lord said to Abraham, 'Why did Sarah laugh and say, "Will I really have a child, now that I am old?" Is anything too hard for the Lord? I will return to you at the appointed time next year and Sarah will have a son.' Sarah was afraid, so she

lied and said, 'I did not laugh.' But he said, 'Yes, you did laugh.'
(Genesis 18:10–15)

It was the custom for married women to stay out of sight of visitors, hence the need in verse 9 to enquire where she is. However,
out of sight she might be, but within earshot she wants to be
and for the first time she hears firsthand the promise of God
concerning her fertility.

Her hushed laughter does not go unnoticed by the heavenly
visitors. It's a dangerous thing to carry on a secret conversation
within your soul in the presence of the Lord. Jesus also surprised his listeners by letting them know that he knew how they
were thinking. Abraham's divine visitor exposes Sarah's hidden
thoughts with the penetrating question, 'Why did Sarah laugh?'
Then God asks the rhetorical question, 'Is anything too difficult for the Lord?' The word 'hard' or 'difficult' (Jeremiah 32:17,
27) is often used to describe God's omnipotence, which is able
to achieve what is unimaginable from a human standpoint, pro-
voking wonder and awe in response (Zechariah 8:6). Surely this
is part of the reason why angelic visitations are experienced
from time to time. For some reason we need to hear, or see, the
unimaginable.

The way this truth is stated, with such simplicity yet with gracious candour, indicates that God expects Sarah to grasp this
truth, and it explains his 'Why?' question to Sarah. God does
not expect our unbelief and inability to comprehend his willingness to act miraculously. He always commends simple and
unquestioning faith (Mark 6:6; 16:14). This same truth is
repeated by the angel to Mary concerning Elizabeth, who,
though barren, conceived in her old age, and to Mary herself,
who will conceive as a virgin. When Mary asks the angel, 'How
will this be?' the angel responds, 'Nothing is impossible with
God' (Luke 1:37).

It is no less a miraculous truth that we hope to share with
unbelievers as we practise hospitality in our homes. As the conversation proceeds there may be opportunities to say something

concerning our faith that will prompt the question 'Why?', to which the answer involves only one explanation: the power of God breaking into our lives bringing salvation.

Sarah can barely take it all in. She is still trying to recover from being exposed in her unbelief. Her only reply to all she has heard is, 'I didn't laugh.' The divine guest transforms her fearful apprehensiveness with a smile: 'But you did laugh.' Laughter inspires the name of her unborn son (Isaac means 'he laughs'), and when he is born she will laugh again. God loves laughter. It's as if God superimposes his smile on her unbelief, and laughter will be born. So Sarah, who thinks she is past experiencing such pleasures, will do so in the birth of this boy and in every subsequent mention of his name.

It's as if God superimposes his smile on her unbelief, and laughter will be born.

Hospitality is always accompanied by laughter. It's a pleasurable thing to be involved in entertaining, and if as a result of shining the light of Jesus in the normal everyday actions of demonstrating care and offering food and wine to strangers there's a new birth (as Jesus called it), there will be endless laughter. And if some of your guests are not angels on this occasion, angels will certainly join in the laughter (Luke 15:7).

What of Abraham's descendants?

With this story as the foundation for the birth of Israel, no Jew should be surprised that God would become flesh and disguise himself as a man. God has been doing that very thing throughout Israel's history. And it shouldn't surprise us that when God came in the person of Jesus, he was always seeking out the most intimate settings to reveal himself to his people.

While many of these occasions took place around meals, it is ironic that Abraham's children showed little hospitality to Jesus. In some homes he was ignored or treated with contempt; in others, like his hometown, he was thrown out. When an enquirer asked to become his disciple, he described his social condition in these poignant words: 'Foxes have holes and birds of the air have nests, but the Son of Man has nowhere to lay his head' (Matthew 8:20). And yet he became everyone else's host, to the point of feeding the five thousand. As he faced death, he hosted a final Passover meal.

Angels: who are they?

It is not within the remit of this book to answer this question fully, but it would be prudent to unpack what we mean by entertaining angels if that is still a potential bonus in our practice of hospitality. The popular image of angels is that they are creatures (both male and female) with large wings and haloes, but that is a relatively narrow understanding from the Scriptures.

The word 'angel' is derived from the Greek word *angelos*, meaning 'messenger'. Let's set out some biblical facts:

1. They are supernatural beings distinctly separate from man (1 Corinthians 6:3; 15:39–41; Hebrews 1:14).
2. They were created by God (Psalm 148:2–5; Colossians 1:16) some time prior to the existence of man (Job 38:7).
3. They provide protection and deliverance from danger (Genesis 19:1,11,15; Psalm 91:11–21; Daniel 6:22; Acts 5:18–19).
4. They serve as a supernatural means of communication between God and man.
5. God uses angels to execute his judgement on the unrighteous (Genesis 19:1–25; 2 Samuel 24:16–17; 2 Kings 19:35; Matthew 13:41–42, 49–50; 24:31; Acts 12:23; Revelation 7:1–2; 8:2–13; 9:15; 15:1).
6. All the angels were created good and holy (Genesis 1:31).
7. Angels will be judged by men (1 Corinthians 6:3), for man was created higher than the angels (Psalm 8:4–5).
8. Angels are not to be worshipped (Colossians 2:18; Hebrews 1:4–5, 13; Revelation 22:8–9).

While the majority of angels referred to are those that are invisible to humankind (Jesus spoke of his angels [Matthew 13:41], his Father's angels [John 1:51], twelve legions of angels [Matthew 26:53]), they frequently appeared during biblical times to carry out God's will. There is no evidence to suggest that they are mindless automatons, but rather, like man, they possess a personality having intellect, emotions and will. The intellect gives them the ability to know and not know certain things (Mark 13:32). They can also reason (1 Peter 1:12). On the morning of the resurrection, the angel that appeared at the tomb spoke openly with Mary Magdalene and the other Mary, instructing them to go and tell the disciples that the Lord had risen and would await their arrival at Galilee (Matthew 28:7).

Angels held a high profile in prophetic events of the past. It was an angel that led Israel out of Egypt (Exodus 14:19), angels were present at the giving of the law at Mount Sinai (Galatians 3:19), and angels assisted Israel in the conquest of the land (Exodus 23:20). And they will play an even more prominent role in the coming day of the Lord. An angel appeared to most of the main characters surrounding Jesus' birth: Mary, Joseph, the shepherds, Zechariah and Simeon. An angel appeared to the women who had come to anoint Jesus' body at the tomb. Furthermore, as God unleashes his wrath in the coming tribulation period, an angel will take a bowl and pour out his anger (Revelation 16:1–2).

The apostle Paul referred to angels about 50 times in his letters. He was always mindful that he was being watched, and lived accordingly: 'We have been made a spectacle to the whole universe, to angels as well as to men' (1 Corinthians 4:9).

Bearing this in mind we are encouraged to understand that the angels of God assist us in the battle against the devil (Hebrews 1:14). One of the New Testament's clearer descriptions of an angelic operation is Peter's escape from prison. An angel appeared to him and temporarily knocked him out. They then escaped from the cell, passed two guards and negotiated a locked iron gate. Once the angel had accomplished all that Peter could not do, he restored Peter's awareness and vanished into the night (Acts 12:5–11).

From this event, and the Old Testament incidents we have referred to, we can learn that there are certainly times when angels interact with us, to warn, encourage and give help in times of need. Whether Peter knew immediately that his rescuer was an angel is not clear; certainly for Abraham there was no knowledge of an angelic visit until later in the day.

Whoever is invited becomes a blessing to the host in numerous ways.

One of the great blessings of hospitality is that whoever is invited becomes a blessing to the host in numerous ways. The sharing of needs and blessings and possibly prayer so often makes us aware that we have been in the presence of God. This is all the more true when our guest is unknown to us and yet has interacted with us in such a way that we have felt encouraged, edified and enriched.

Back in Genesis 18 and 19, after the angelic visitors have eaten, rested and given Abraham and Sarah the news that after waiting many years Sarah will finally bear a son, they prepare to leave for Sodom and Gomorrah. Some pretty ungodly behaviour by the men of Sodom follows. As a result God says that the outcry against Sodom is great and their sin is grave, but he does not say what the sin is. I was taught that the sin for which Sodom was destroyed was homosexuality, hence the word 'sodomy'. But that sin is never mentioned in the context of Sodom. Isaiah refers to Sodom twice, but only mentions the sin of injustice (Isaiah 1:10; 3:9); Jeremiah mentions a host of irresponsible acts (Jeremiah 23:14) and Ezekiel is quite specific about the city's sin, naming pride, gluttony and neglecting the needy. What is more interesting for us is that Jesus mentions these cities and their ungodliness when speaking on the subject of hospitality:

'Whatever town or village you enter, search for some worthy person there and stay at his house until you leave. As you enter the home, give it your greeting. If the home is deserving, let your peace rest on it; if it is not, let your peace return to you. If anyone will not welcome you or listen to your words, shake the dust off your feet when you leave that home or town. I tell you the truth, it will be more bearable for Sodom and Gomorrah on the day of judgment than for that town.' (Matthew 10:11–16)

Whatever else the sin of Sodom was, it was certainly a failure to enact justice and practise the hospitality God demanded. Clearly Jesus is speaking in a culture where to turn up on an unfamiliar doorstep would normally be greeted with unquestioned hospitality, and he gives his disciples the fullest encouragement to proceed in this manner with the good news of Jesus.

We don't live in that culture, but there is something in the phrase 'if the home is deserving' that makes me ponder about the worthiness of my home in the context of my willingness to accept the message of God. The Greek word translated 'deserving' here is from the word *axios*, meaning 'of weight', or more correctly 'weighted against another object'. The picture is that of two objects on a pair of scales. The word 'deserving' or 'worthy' is always used in Scripture in the context of God's character in some way. So to walk 'worthy of our calling' (Ephesians 4:1) is to put our walk on one side of the scales and God's call on our life on the other and see if they balance or not. Belshazzar's life was weighed on the scales and found wanting (Daniel 5:27).

The challenge here is that our lives and homes are worthy and that unlike Belshazzar's life or the people of Sodom and Gomorrah, we are not found wanting.

PUTTING PRINCIPLES INTO PRACTICE:

1. At what point did Abraham realise he had entertained angels? Would he have done things any differently if he had known they were coming?

2. Have you ever had an experience where you genuinely felt, after the event, that an angel was involved? Describe your feelings at the time and after the event.

3. Does the possibility that we might, as Paul implies, entertain angels without being aware of it make you want to
   entertain strangers more, or begin to do so? Give the
   reasons for your answer.
4. Read Psalm 91. Should we expect to experience angelic
   activity? How do you think you would recognise angels if
   you encountered them?

Notes

1. Ancient Customs

1. Harvey Lutske, *The Book of Jewish Customs* (Northvale, New Jersey: Jason Aronson Inc., 1986), p. 321.
2. Homer, *The Odyssey* (Garden City, New York: Doubleday,1961), p. 233, translated by Robert Fitzgerald.
3. Lactantius, *The Divine Institutes*, bk 6, ch.12, The Ante-Nicene Fathers (ed. Roberts and Donaldson), (Edinburgh:T&T Clark, 1867–72), vol. 7, p. 176.

2. Starting Relationships

1. Christine D. Pohl, *Making Room – Recovering Hospitality as a Christian Tradition* (Grand Rapids: Wm B. Eerdmans, 1999), p. 41.
2. Taken from the website: www.ezrabessaroth.org

3. Building Relationships

1. Lucien Richard, O.M.I. *Living the Hospitality of God* (New Jersey: Paulist Press, 2000), p. 7.
2. Rosemary Haughton, 'Hospitality: home as the integra-

tion of privacy and community', in Lucien Richard, *op cit.*, p. 11.

3. Martin Luther, *Luther's Works*, vol. 3: Lectures on Genesis, chapters 15–20 (St Louis: Concordia, 1961), p. 189.

4. Peter Farb and George Armelagos, *Consuming Passions: the Anthropology of Eating* (Boston: Houghton Mifflin, 1980), pp. 158–9.

5. Donald Altman, *Art of the Inner Meal* (SanFrancisco: Harper, 2000), p. 5f.

6. Peter Maurin, *Easy Essays* (New York: Sheed & Ward, 1936), p. 46.

7. Barbara Roche MP, in a GMTV interview, 11th December 2002.

8. Alexander Kinglake, 'Eothen', in Jeremy Paxman, *The English* (London: Penguin Books Ltd, 1999), p. 116.

4. Prioritising Relationships

1. John Mallison, *Mentoring to Develop Disciples and Leaders* (Scripture Union/Openbook Publishers Australia, 1998), p. 8.

2. John Wesley, *General Rules for Methodist Fellowships* (1743), taken from the Internet.

5. Friendship Evangelism

1. John Calvin, *Commentaries on the Epistle of Paul the Apostle to the Hebrews* (Grand Rapids: Wm B. Eerdmans, 1948), p. 340.

2. Gene Edwards, *How to Meet in Homes* (Seed Sowers USA, 1969), p. 59.

3. Christine D. Pohl, *op. cit.*, p. 43.

4. *Ibid*, p. 57.

5. Martin Luther, *Luther's Works* vol. 4, Lectures on Genesis, chapters 21–25 (Philadelphia: Fortress, 1955), p. 282.

6. Christine D. Pohl, *op cit.*, p. 96.

7. Who is my Neighbour?

1. John Wesley, *Works of John Wesley*, Vol. 3, Sermon 98: 'On Visiting The Sick' (Nashville: Abingdon, 1986), pp. 387f.
2. Peter C. Wagner, *Churches That Pray* (Regal Books, 1993), p. 207.

9. Strangers on our Shores

1. William Woodward, quoted by Dorothy R. Rape in the American magazine *His* (October 1979).
2. Catherine Weston, *Welcoming International Students in Your Church* (Friends International).
3. R. Max Kershaw, *How to Share the Good News with Your Muslim Friend* (Colorado Springs, Co: International Students, Inc., 1971, 1990), p. 3.
4. *Ibid*, p. 23.
5. Ron and Patty McCulloch, *Hints for Hosts*, Friends International leaflet.
6. David Pargeter, taken from the Internet (www.pastornet. net.au/jmm/aame).
7. Rabbi Jonathan Sacks, 'You shall also love the stranger', taken from the Internet.
8. Hon. George Carey, 'Christmas Day Sermon 2000', Canterbury Cathedral, taken from the Internet.
9. Christine D. Pohl, *op cit*., p. 52.
10. Home Office and Refugee Council statistics.

10. Entertaining Angels

1. Roland de Vaux, *Ancient Israel* (London: Darton, Longman & Todd, 1961), p. 202.